TAKING CHARGE THROUGH HOME SCHOOLING

TAKING CHARGE

THROUGH HOME SCHOOLING:

PERSONAL AND POLITICAL

EMPOWERMENT

M. Larry and Susan D. Kaseman

Koshkonong Press
Stoughton, Wisconsin

Publisher's Cataloging in Publication

Kaseman, M. Larry
    Taking charge through home schooling : personal
and political empowerment / M. Larry and Susan D.
Kaseman. --
    p.   cm.
    Includes bibliographical references and index.
    ISBN 0-9628365-0-8

    1. Home schooling--United States. 2. Home schooling--
Law and legislation. I. Kaseman, Susan D., II. Title.

LC40.K3 1990   649.68
                                QBI90-58
                                MARC

This edition printed in the United States
of America. First printing September, 1990.
Second printing April, 1991.

Important note: Nothing in this book is
intended or should be taken as the giving of legal
advice. This book is not intended to substitute
for privately retained legal counsel.

Dedicated to

Elizabeth
Peter
Gretchen
Megan

who made it possible.

Acknowledgments

We want to express our appreciation to:

Our parents

> Meg Gilmore
> Bob Gilmore
> Katherine Kaseman Ritchie
> and the late Milbert L. Kaseman

Members of Wisconsin Parents Association

The people who got us started

> Suzy
> Erin
> Amy
> Levi
> Mike

Authors we have read and

La Leche League and its members.

CONTENTS

INTRODUCTION

Home schooling will change your life. People who home school, even briefly, are profoundly affected by the experience. Few things have the hold on our lives that schooling does. Yet home schooling can break the bonds of conventional schooling. Home schooling changes lives as

--Children discover alternative ways of thinking, learning, and solving problems.

--Children who hated school recover the delight in learning that they had as toddlers but lost in a bureaucratic institution.

--Children who were labeled "learning disabled" or "hyperactive" or "ADD" discover they can learn well in a more flexible environment with loving support from their parents.

--Parents who disliked school or felt like failures or were abused there reclaim their own joy in learning and discover that they can do many of the things that a conventional school once told them they were incapable of doing.

--Parents who did well in school find that there is more joy and complexity in learning than they ever realized and that in many ways they have been handicapped by their school "success." Through working and learning with their children, they themselves recover the ability to learn freely, to try new things without fear of failure, and to think for themselves rather than to recite what a teacher wants to hear.

1

--Families who take responsibility for safeguarding their freedom to home school discover that they can have control over their own lives and that they do not need to rely on "experts." They communicate with legislators, counter unjust attempts at regulation by school officials, and become part of a grassroots movement to strengthen the role and function of the family in our society.

No one who begins home schooling walks away from the experience unchanged. Those who home school for only a short time find they then view conventional schools differently, as just one option rather than as a necessity. Families who home school for longer periods and feel positively about it, are affected even more strongly. One simply cannot undertake an activity that society says must be done by professionals in a special building and do it in one's own home (often with fewer problems and greater satisfaction than "experts" in an institution provide) without being powerfully affected by the experience.

Often the families who benefit most from home schooling are those who view the experience in its totality. They question basic assumptions about learning and search for their own answers and alternative ways of learning. They see how home schooling relates to their principles and beliefs. They are willing to assume their share of the responsibility for home schooling laws and regulations in their state, to join with other home schoolers to fight any unjust law or regulation, to act carefully in ways that will not allow opponents of home schooling an opportunity to increase regulation.

This book seeks to empower readers by describing alternatives and showing how they can be exercised. Alternatives exist throughout life, but if we do not know what our choices are, we do not have any. Empowerment includes identifying options and realizing that we can make choices and act on them, that we can take charge. No one else can make these decisions for us as well as we can make them for ourselves (although others will certainly try).

The first aim of this book is to help people take charge of their own learning by exploring alternative approaches to learning and choosing the ones that work for them. Part I supports parents who are considering or beginning home schooling by providing perspective, responding to common concerns, and suggesting ways of dealing with special circumstances. Part II questions conventional ideas about learning and presents alternative approaches. Also discussed are ways of handling daily challenges, from providing a supportive learning environment to finding time for oneself. Ideas about high school at home are included.

The second aim of this book is to increase awareness of the political nature of everyday actions and of ways of becoming empowered through them. To regain and maintain our freedom, we must realize both that we have to be politically active and that we are very capable of doing just that. Part III discusses the political context in which educational freedom is determined and the crosscurrents that are swirling around us. It sheds light on opposition to home schooling, contributions we could make as home schoolers, and challenges facing the home schooling movement.

Following this overview, the book focuses on the foundations, principles, and practical aspects of political actions people can take. Part IV discusses ways of assessing the political situation in a state and then improving the climate for home schooling. It includes options for changing educational policy, ways of forming and participating in a grassroots organization, and ideas for working with the media.

Home schooling laws are discussed in Part V. Empowerment comes through reading and interpreting laws, understanding and using arguments that support favorable laws and counter restrictive ones, and working with the legislature to gain and maintain reasonable laws. Part VI presents ways of making the best of current laws, including maintaining rights and dealing effectively with public officials.

If we are to maximize our strength and maintain our freedoms, we must work together. Therefore, the third aim of this book is to foster unity (not uniformity) among home schoolers so that this movement, about which we care deeply and to which we are strongly committed, stands a better chance of not being be co-opted by either the educational establishment or self-appointed "experts" and leaders from within the home schooling community. We must work together to regain and maintain the rights each of us has to make our own decisions about alternatives in education and about religious and moral beliefs. We must respect the right of each person to make his own decisions in these matters. By working together, we are in the best position to protect the freedom of parents to choose for their children an education consistent with their principles and beliefs. Without this freedom we would all be less than we can be with it, for it allows us to decide about things more important than politics, about learning, and religion, and principles and beliefs.

Take this book in the spirit in which it is offered. Use the parts that are helpful to you and skip the rest. Consider reading it with pencil in hand; underline, cross out, add your own ideas and comments. To assist you with this, the book is formatted in the style of a manual. There are lists of ideas, options, and suggestions along with many cross references. Some repetition is inevitable as the book tries to present, in linear form, ideas which are interconnected. As another aspect of style, the use of "he" and "she" is alternated by paragraph to include everyone and avoid the awkwardness of "he or she."

We are delighted that you are reading about one of the most exciting ways in which people are experiencing personal and political empowerment. May your encounter with home schooling be enriching and rewarding.

Larry and Susan Kaseman
Stoughton, Wisconsin
April, 1991

PART I

BEGINNING HOME SCHOOLING

CHAPTER 1

DECIDING TO HOME SCHOOL

The purpose of this chapter is not to convince you to home school. Rather it is to provide some information that may help you decide whether or not to home school. Some of the suggestions may also assist your thinking and planning if you choose this alternative.

WHY HOME SCHOOL

The decision to home school involves much more than where a child will learn to read and do long division. It is a big responsibility with serious consequences. It is also an adventure. People decide to home school for many reasons and in different ways. Some decide intellectually that it will provide the best education for their child. Others are led through prayer or feel in their hearts that it is right for them. Still others reluctantly choose it as the best alternative, although they lack confidence in their own abilities or are reluctant for some other reason. Parents' feelings about home schooling vary, too. Many embrace it joyfully and truly love it. Some begin out of a sense of duty and find they like it better than they had expected, while others persist only because they are convinced it is best for their children.

Among the strengths and advantages of home schooling are the following: A child can learn at his own pace, when he is ready, using the learning styles and approaches that work for him.

Without the limitations of a conventional classroom, he can pursue special interests in depth; think creatively; and make the most of his strengths, abilities, and talents. Within the security of his own home and family, he can work one-on-one with a parent who cares deeply about him and gives him strong support. He does not have to contend with either the competition and peer pressure of a classroom or the stress of trying to learn something before he is ready. He has the opportunity to learn from direct experience with the real world, to interact with a wide range of people of different ages, to be of service to others, to participate in real activities that make sense, and to discover how to learn in his own way. A home schooling parent has much more control over his child's environment and is able to provide important support. A parent also has many opportunities to learn with her child and through home schooling.

SHOULD OUR FAMILY HOME SCHOOL?

Many parents consider questions such as the following:

--What are my major reasons for considering home schooling?

--In what ways would home schooling benefit my child? How would it be detrimental? How would attending a conventional school benefit my child? How would it be detrimental?

--How would home schooling affect our family life? Our family budget? My child's relationships with his friends? Our relationships with people outside the family? The work being done by adults in the family?

--Would it make more sense for my child to spend her time, energy, and resources learning at home or going to school? Would it make more sense for me to spend my time, energy, and resources (including money) to home school or to support my child's attendance at a conventional school?

--Would home schooling or attending a conventional school be a better way for my child to learn, for example, each of the following (add anything you want to):
>   --basic academic skills?
>   --how to learn?
>   --religious and moral values?
>   --how to get along with peers and with people of different ages?
>   --how to master a skill that interests him?
>   --how to assume responsibility and get a job done?
>   --appreciation of natural beauty and the arts?

--Are there important lessons or opportunities that my child will miss if she does not attend a conventional school? If so, are there ways I could compensate?

--Are there important lessons or opportunities that my child will miss if he attends a conventional school rather than a home school? If so, could I compensate?

--What stresses and tensions would my child face in home schooling? In attending a conventional school? Which of these would he be better able to handle? Where would my child find the most supportive environment?

--What are my biggest concerns or worries about home schooling? With whom could I discuss them?

COMMON CONCERNS OF PROSPECTIVE HOME SCHOOLERS

How will I find time to teach my child or children? Home schooling does take time, but it is often much more manageable than non-home schoolers assume. Different approaches to learning require varying amounts of time. A child involved in learner-led learning (which is described in Chapter 4) may require less of a parent's time that might be expected. Many parents feel that children benefit from some unplanned time during which they can decide what they want to do. Some children participate in their parent's activities, learning in this way to repair cars, cook, sew, garden, etc. and sometimes reducing the parent's workload as well. It takes a lot of time (and energy) to send a child to school, and many families find that time is more manageable (and more pleasant) when they home school. In short, many parents like home schooling; they give their time freely and willingly and receive rich rewards. (For ideas about parents' finding time for themselves, see pp. 65-67.)

Is home schooling expensive? Not necessarily. Many families manage creatively with simple basic resources and a lot of ingenuity. Resources such as libraries (see p. 31) are available at little or no cost. For some families a major factor is the loss of income when one or both parents choose to be home more. (However, given the costs of earning money, including transportation, clothes, higher taxes, increased food costs, child care, etc., it is difficult for the second parent to earn much, so the loss is sometimes not as great as might be expected.). Some parents willingly trade what they could be earning for the rewards of being at home with their children, and others work at home. Home schoolers save the costs of schooling, which can include tuition, transportation, supplies, clothes, lunches, and many incidentals.

What if I do not know something my child wants or needs to learn? Many resources are available, and you can learn yourself and then share it with your child, or learn with your child, or assist her in finding resources (books, tutors, formal courses, etc.) so she can learn without your direct involvement.

How will I know if my child is learning enough, if he is up to grade level, if I am doing a good enough job? You will have many opportunities to observe your child and get a general sense of what he is learning. Many home schooling parents question the whole idea of grade levels, feeling that they are a construct that does not do justice to the individuality and strengths of a child. Even if grade levels did make sense, a child's grade level cannot be accurately determined because there is no way to measure accurately what a person knows (tests measure how good one is at taking tests, not how much one knows). For more ideas on evaluating a child's learning, see pp. 47-49.

Other concerns of home schooling parents, whether new or experienced, are discussed in Chapter 6.

WHAT ARE THE LEGAL REQUIREMENTS FOR HOME SCHOOLING?

One way to begin finding out about legal requirements in your state is to contact a state or local home schooling organization or talk with several home schoolers. The national home schooling publications listed in the Appendix have directories of state organizations and/or individuals. Comparing information from several different sources is probably a good idea. Among the questions you might ask are:

--What are the basic legal requirements for home schooling? How can I get a copy of them? Are they enforced by local school districts or by the state bureaucracy (or department of education) or both? Do public officials and home schoolers disagree about how the laws and regulations should be interpreted and enforced? Do most home schoolers fulfill the legal requirements? How vigorously are they enforced? What are the penalties for non-compliance? What is your recommendation to me concerning compliance with requests by the state?

--Are there pending home schooling issues, such as proposed or threatened legislation or court cases in progress? What do you expect to happen and when? Are there things that I might inadvertently do or say that might jeopardize what home schoolers are trying to accomplish? How do I avoid doing these things?

Do not assume that you have to do something just because someone (such as a school official) tells you that you must.

11

Officials sometimes may tell you to do what they would like you to do, even though it is not required by law. Also, differences often exist between the way school officials and home schoolers interpret laws and regulations, and home schoolers' interpretations may be more valid than those of the officials.

Secure a copy of the laws and regulations that apply to home schoolers, which may include laws concerning private schools, compulsory school attendance, truancy, immunization, and other topics. You may be able to get copies from a home schooling organization or a support group, or you can look them up yourself at a public library, law library, or court house. (Check the index for "home schooling," "private schools," "compulsory school attendance," "truancy," etc.) You can also ask your state legislator to send you a copy of the laws and regulations, but unless your request is very specific, you may not get copies of all the relevant laws and regulations, so it may be better to do the research yourself. Read them yourself so you know exactly what is required. Think about ways these requirements could be interpreted. Find out their history, including the intent of the legislature when it passed the laws. For more information on reading and interpreting laws, see pp. 197-201.

Be cautious about contacting the state department of education or local school officials for information. They may give you incomplete information and misleading interpretations, and some of them track people who ask for information on home schooling. Many people avoid contacting school officials unless it is absolutely necessary, and then they do so only after at least two or three home schoolers have convinced them of the necessity and wisdom of doing this.

ADDITIONAL CONSIDERATIONS

A home schooling parent assumes a very serious responsibility. In addition to meeting legal requirements, parents consider questions such as:

--What are my goals for my child's education? See pp. 15-17.

--How will I evaluate my child's progress toward these goals? See pp. 47-49.

--How will adequate supervision be provided for my child? A parent at home full time is one of the most common approaches, of course, but there are other options, depending on the age and abilities of the child, family circumstances, etc.

--How will I provide adequate social interaction for my child? Learning to interact with a variety of people of different ages is commonly recognized as an important part of growing up. Many parents find that home schooling makes it easier for a child to have meaningful contact with people of different ages. Contact with peers comes through neighborhood activities, organized sports, youth organizations such as Scouts, 4-H, and church groups. On the other hand, the interaction of 25 children in a classroom can have negative aspects such as intense competition and peer dependency. This leads many parents to feel that the social aspects of a classroom setting need not be duplicated and in fact may best be avoided. After all, school is the only place people are required to interact with a group of people who are all the same age.

--What community resources are available and how will I use them as part of my child's education? Much depends on opportunities available in the community; a child's interests and abilities; and a parent's imagination, time schedule, and willingness to chauffeur. Many parents seek opportunities for their children to serve as well as to be served. Also, home schooling support groups are a valuable resource.

--How will I provide my child learning resources in an environment that supports learning? See pp. 17-18 for suggestions for deciding on a curriculum, pp. 27-46 for information on alternative approaches to learning, pp. 54-57 for ideas about learning environments, and the Appendix for a list of suggested resources.

--How can I protect my child and our home school from unnecessary regulation by the state? This requires that a parent be politically active. For more information, see pp. 87-103.

REASSURING PERSPECTIVES

Parents who are seriously considering home schooling but also have doubts may want to consider the following:

--Of course home schooling involves risks, but sending a child to a conventional school is not risk-free, since problems and negative experiences are not uncommon there.

--Learning is a lifelong process. If a brief home schooling experience does not work out for your family, your child has time to catch up. At the same time, if you do not try home schooling, you will miss the opportunities, strengths, and advantages of this approach.

--You do not have to make a long commitment to home schooling. Many children home school for a time and then enter or re-enter a conventional school. Some parents feel that even a brief experience with home schooling is valuable; children then view school differently, realizing that there are alternative ways to learn and that school is an option, not a necessity. There is the chance that you will decide to stop home schooling only to find that your child likes it so well that she resists school. In such a situation, however, the child's determination often gives her parents the incentive they need to overcome whatever problems they were having with home schooling.

--For many parents, home schooling is a matter of heart and belief; they feel deeply and strongly that they should be home schooling. They sometimes start home schooling with only this conviction to go on, unsure of exactly how they will proceed, and they work out practical details and solve problems as they go.

14

CHAPTER 2

GOALS AND CURRICULUMS

POSSIBLE GOALS AND OBJECTIVES FOR A HOME SCHOOL

The following list is only suggestions; each family or student needs to select what is most important. Check items that interest you or seem right, ignore the others, and add anything else you want to include.

BASIC ACADEMIC GOALS

--Learn to read and understand books, newspapers, magazines, etc. well enough to get information you need and to be able to read for enjoyment.

--Learn to write well enough to be able to clarify your thinking, record important ideas and events, and communicate with others.

--Learn to speak well enough to be able to present yourself and your ideas to others in a small group, a public meeting, etc.

--Learn basic mathematics well enough to be able to handle money, solve everyday problems, avoid being cheated, and see something of the underlying structure and beauty of the world of numbers.

--Develop an understanding and appreciation of other countries and cultures.

--Develop a sense of history, of the progression of time and the order in which major events occurred, and of the process of change in human society.

--Learn how societies are organized and how governments operate.

--Develop an appreciation of nature and its beauty and a sense of the processes by which nature operates.

--Learn enough basic science to be able to understand the background of some of the moral dilemmas facing modern Americans.

--Learn to speak and read a second language.

--Learn to play a musical instrument, compose music, enjoy listening.

PRACTICAL SKILLS

--Learn how to get and responsibly hold a job.
--Learn to cook, clean, and run a household.
--Learn to manage money effectively.
--Learn to drive and care for an automobile.
--Learn to take responsibility for your health.
--Learn to type.
--Learn to sew, knit, crochet, weave, etc.

MORAL AND RELIGIOUS VALUES

--Learn to maintain close, satisfying, responsible relationships with other people.

--Learn to live and work effectively as a member of a community.

--Develop ethical principles and distinguish between right and wrong.

--Learn the beliefs and history of the religious group to which you belong.

--Learn to use resources responsibly and wisely.

--Develop an appreciation for beauty.

--Learn to be a responsible citizen.

DECIDING ON A CURRICULUM AND SELECTING OTHER RESOURCES

A curriculum is an educational plan, a way of achieving one's educational goals and objectives. A home school curriculum can be tailored to meet a child's interests, abilities, and needs. There is no one right or best approach. Each family must decide for itself what is most important and what works best.

Some families follow the curriculum used by their local public school; some use one of the numerous prepared curriculums available; some work with a correspondence or satellite school; some develop their own curriculum. Many home schoolers find it works well to carefully consider each child; decide on goals and priorities; read about available alternatives; talk with other home schoolers; visit the vendor area at a home schooling conference or attend a curriculum fair; and then begin. For more information about resources, see the Appendix.

Be prepared to try a number of different approaches until you find what works well for you and your child. Often different children in the same family benefit from different approaches. Discard what does not work and build on what does. Be prepared to continue making changes as your child grows. Remember that educators consistently give high marks to a tutorial approach in which each student works individually with a tutor; that is what home schooling is. Exploring various approaches to learning, curriculums, and resources is one of the most exciting parts of home education, for parents as well as children, and children (and parents) learn much from the search.

Books about home schooling are helpful to many parents. Practical how-to books may provide specific ideas. Theories about how children learn may assist parents in choosing the direction they want to take and the approach they want to use. Information about the legal basis for home schooling and parents' rights may give parents more confidence in talking with others about home schooling. Stories of home schooling families may comfort, amuse, and inspire. See the Appendix for titles of suggested books about home schooling.

CHAPTER 3

SPECIAL CIRCUMSTANCES

BEGINNING DURING THE HIGH SCHOOL YEARS

High school at home is just another stage of home schooling, one which many families find richly rewarding. However, there are fewer high school age home schoolers than younger children. Less information is available about high school at home than about the earlier years. More parents feel somewhat overwhelmed and intimidated. Some alternatives are discussed in Chapter 8 to help a family choose its own approach.

A teen beginning home schooling after a negative experience in a conventional school may benefit from a chance to relax, unwind, and take a break from conventional school work while participating in other worthwhile activities such as learning a new craft, interacting with elderly people, repairing an engine, or developing a physical skill. Taking time to explore the world and pursue established interests or develop new ones can help a teen's confidence, self-esteem, and sense of direction.

HOME SCHOOLING A CHILD WHO HAS BEEN LABELED

A child who has been labeled "learning disabled," "hyperactive," "minimally brain damaged," "emotionally disturbed," "ADD," etc. has often had such a negative school experience that beginning home schooling presents special challenges, especially since school personnel may try hard to convince parents that they are not qualified to teach their child and that the only hope is to turn him over to the "experts" at school. However, many parents of children who have been labeled report that home schooling solved many problems and allowed them to grow and learn in amazing ways.

The first step in resolving such a situation is often the parent's realization that labels are frequently wrong. Sometimes children are misdiagnosed. The tests and techniques used to label children have been shown to be highly questionable. Despite extensive research, no clear evidence exists that children labeled "learning disabled" actually have neurological or other physiological problems. It seems much more likely that difficulties in learning are caused by a combination of factors, including the stresses and tensions of school, pressure on children to learn before they are ready, not encouraging children to use learning styles or approaches that suit them best, attempts to teach children material they find boring or irrelevant, children's lack of experiences the teacher assumes they have had, problems of poverty and lack of resources, and so forth.

We all have difficulties in learning at times, and some children have more difficulty than others in learning what is expected in a school setting. But having difficulty in learning does not mean one has a "learning disability." Schools often find it to their benefit to label children, partly because they then get extra federal and state funding. Special education is the area which is expanding most rapidly in conventional schools, generating new jobs, programs, and facilities. Also schools can then blame the children rather than asking if the school system itself is flawed.

Even if there were a clearly identifiable deficiency within some children that prevented their learning, it could still be said that labeling is wrong in the sense that the school is taking a negative and self-defeating approach to the problem. When someone is having difficulty, a supportive, nurturing person does not say, "Well, no wonder--you have a disability so you are not able to learn that." How much better to say, "You seem to be having trouble learning this right now. Do you want to try a different way of doing it or set it aside for a while?"

Parents who have any lingering doubts that perhaps the school was right when it labeled their child, may find it helpful to read Lori and Bill Granger's *Magic Feather*. The authors describe their experiences when their son was labeled, show how and why schools often mislabel and misdiagnose, stress the importance of the parents' role in protecting their children from labeling, and offer support and suggestions for what parents can do.

Many parents make it clear to their child and to other people that the school was wrong. They express confidence in their child and her abilities. They deal with their feelings but do not waste a lot of time on anger or guilt. Instead they move on from where they are now.

Many parents find it works well to begin home schooling with activities different from the conventional school assignments, workbooks, and tests that were causing their child trouble. Worthwhile learning activities include doing arts and crafts, listening while someone reads aloud from books a child enjoys, cooking, playing music, developing physical skills, gardening, visiting interesting people, doing volunteer work, and playing all sorts of games. Some families feel that imaginative play is a valuable experience. Limiting or eliminating television and encouraging a child to pursue what interests him often work well.

After home schooling for a while, many children are more relaxed and have regained some of their natural curiosity and desire to learn. Many problems resolve themselves, without anyone's making a deliberate effort to solve them, once a child is

21

no longer under pressure to perform at a certain level. Parents are amazed at how much children learn easily and happily. Many parents also take advantage of this opportunity to help their child see how much ability she has and to boost her self-esteem.

These activities often eventually draw a child into more conventional learning activities when he wants to read about a topic of particular interest, learn more math so he can use it as a tool for some project, or write about what he is doing or thinking. Parents who feel this learning is not happening quickly enough, of course, can gently steer their child in this direction. A book like Thomas Armstrong's *In Their Own Way* or John Holt's *Learning All the Time* can increase a parent's awareness of all the different ways in which children learn and in which parents can assist them.

HOME SCHOOLING A HANDICAPPED CHILD

Parents of a child who is blind, deaf, or has other physical handicaps also face special challenges. As in the case of children who have been labeled "learning disabled," schools often try to convince parents that their child must be in school to receive the benefit of the "expert" assistance available only there. However, many parents find that not only are they very capable of home schooling their handicapped child, but also the child does much better at home than in school. This is no doubt in part because of one-to-one attention he receives from loving parents, reduced pressures and stresses, and opportunities to learn in a wider variety of ways than schools encourage or allow.

HOME SCHOOLING A CHILD WHO HAS HAD TRUANCY PROBLEMS IN A CONVENTIONAL SCHOOL

Here again beginning home schoolers have reason for optimism--many children who find school so intolerable that they become truants end up learning well and happily at home. Many parents give their child a chance to regain her equilibrium by substituting alternative learning activities for the conventional school requirements, textbooks, workbooks, and tests that may have been causing their child difficulty. A child can learn a great deal by doing arts and crafts, reading books she really enjoys, studying music, developing physical skills, gardening, visiting interesting people, and doing volunteer work. Some parents limit or eliminate television during this time and otherwise encourage a child to pursue what interests her.

Parents of these children may face three special challenges. First, the child may have been labeled a "law breaker" or "criminal" and heard dire predictions made about his future. Such a picture of oneself is unsettling, to say the least, and may become a self-fulfilling prophecy unless someone is able to help the child change it. Some parents view truancy as an indication that there is something wrong with the school system rather than with their child and are able to convey this to their child and help him make a realistic assessment of his strengths, abilities, and potential.

Second, unlike most parents (who freely choose home schooling and begin enthusiastically), parents of these children may feel they are being forced into something they do not want to undertake, are not fully capable of doing, and do not have time to do. Parents who respond positively at this time to their child's genuine needs are often richly rewarded. They sometimes use their relief at having the truancy question settled to bring creative energy to their home schooling venture. They figure out things they can do with their child that both of them will enjoy. They work with their child on learning projects. In addition to the satisfaction of seeing improvement in their child, they end up liking home schooling better than they anticipated.

Third, because of the history of truancy problems, school officials may scrutinize or harass such a family more than other home schooling families in the district. Some families deal with this by knowing what the law requires, complying carefully, and standing their ground firmly but politely in contacts with school officials. (See pp. 250-256 for more information on dealing with school officials.) Some also minimize the opportunities officials have to contact them by appearing as conventional as possible without compromising important principles. For example, they are careful that their child is clearly being supervised and is doing something educational during conventional school hours. They explain their home schooling program to neighbors, relatives or others who might be concerned; this may help minimize contacts with officials.

PART II

LEARNING EVERY DAY

CHAPTER 4

ALTERNATIVE APPROACHES TO LEARNING

It is unfortunate that this chapter exists. Learning is a natural activity. We are born knowing how. Ideally we would simply continue to learn throughout our lives, not giving much thought to the process, not worrying about it--just learning as we live. That is how it probably is in some cultures. Not in ours, however. Our society institutionalizes learning, tries to direct and control it, and thereby distorts and sometimes even ruins it. Because learning is one of home schoolers' major goals, and because home schoolers are often asked what their children are learning and/or required to show what their children are learning, it often helps for home schoolers to begin by trying to identify and clarify some of their assumptions and beliefs about learning.

It is also unfortunate that this chapter exists because reading about learning is not the best way to learn about it. Better ways are to learn something ourselves and observe our reactions and to watch people around us as they learn, too. But for most of our lives most of us have been told that the only real learning is conventional learning (for example, reading a textbook and taking a test on it, or filling in a math workbook, or doing a series of specifically prescribed experiments designed to lead a learner to "discover" a scientific principle). It is time that more authors told us that there are alternatives to conventional learning, so that as we are observing learning we might be on the look out for them.

Also, as we observe and explore, an occasional book can provide reassuring support and a few insights or clarifications; so it is in the spirit of sharing that this chapter is offered.

EXAMINING YOUR ASSUMPTIONS ABOUT LEARNING AND EDUCATION

Our culture has many assumptions about learning. By examining these and alternatives to them, we can get a clearer idea of what we are trying to do in home schooling. It becomes easier to choose an approach to learning that will suit our family. We can become empowered and take charge of our home school. Some of these assumptions are so deep seated that we may find we unintentionally act on them, even though we know they are inaccurate or extreme. Some make home schooling (or any other approach to learning) much more difficult than it need be. It may be a good idea occasionally to hold them up to the light of day, examine them critically, save the ones that are worth it, and discard those that are unnecessary or causing too much trouble.

Some of these assumptions are fundamental to the approach to education chosen by conventional schools. Reviewing them can provide new insights on conflicts between school officials and home schoolers. Also, some assumptions (such as requiring children to sit quietly in their seats) have been adopted because they make it easier to manage a group of 20 or so children, even though they do not foster learning and in fact may interfere with it. Examining these assumptions may help home schoolers avoid unnecessary and potentially harmful practices.

Some of the ideas on this list may be new to you, some may seem outlandish, some you may strongly disagree with. Take them in the spirit in which they are offered: ponder the ones that appeal to you and ignore the ones that do not. Allow yourself time--time to learn about learning, which takes some of us a while, especially if we were conventionally schooled ourselves.

--Our culture seems to assume that people do most of their learning (at least the part that really matters) within a school building between the ages of five or six to 16 or 18 or 22. An alternative view holds that learning is a lifelong process most of which takes place outside a school building, which is an artificial and rather sterile environment. It is easy to give a quick nod to lifelong learning, more difficult to consider what it really means, for the idea that people should study for about 12 years and then start living is more deeply seated in our culture than many people realize. Lifelong learning is more than an occasional adult education course. It is the expectation that someone will know more at age 40 than she did at age 30, the realization that it is never too late to begin learning another language, the belief that there are important new insights just over the horizon, no matter how old you are. But it is easy to forget these things, and a great deal of pressure on a home schooler results from the perhaps unintentional assumption that everything a child will need to know during his life must be mastered in his first 18 years.

--The idea that people must be taught, must receive formal or informal instruction from someone, in order to learn is another deep seated assumption that home schooling parents have to deal with. Do children really need to be taught? If so, what subjects, at what age, in what way? But if this is the case, how do children learn two very difficult skills, walking and talking, without anyone's making a self-conscious effort to teach them? Could children learn other things, even "school" subjects like reading and math, in the same way, by imitating other people's behavior, making mistakes, correcting them by themselves, and asking for help when they need it?

--A standardized curriculum is based on the assumption that it contains the material that an educated person needs to know and that by mastering it, one will be prepared for life. Such curriculums were devised to make it manageable for one teacher to educate many children at the same time, but their existence promotes this assumption. An alternative approach points out that each person is a unique individual, and that it is impossible to learn, remember, and use everything there is to know, so each learner inevitably misses important knowledge. Therefore a person should have an individualized curriculum (that is, an educational plan or a general idea of what he wants to learn, not necessarily a formal, written document) based on his own personal strengths, interests, abilities, and needs. Each person should have some say, even a lot of say, in what his curriculum includes. Is he not perhaps the best judge of it? At any rate, he is certainly the one who will have to do the work involved.

--Another assumption is that a learner has to begin at the beginning of a subject and proceed in a certain sequence, being careful not to miss any steps along the way, an idea that either supports or is fostered by standardized curriculums. An alternative approach is simply to plunge in, begin at any convenient point, make sense of what you can and not worry about the rest, continue exploring, and let the pieces gradually fall into place. This is, in fact, how people learn much of what they know that does not come from formalized instruction. It can be inefficient, but it can also be very exciting, allow the learner to make her own discoveries, stimulate new thinking, sustain her interest, and in the long run be more productive.

--Closely related is the idea that children should study material carefully prepared for their level. Of course there is subject matter that is inappropriate for children, but within a given subject, children often respond more positively to adult-level material; it is more interesting and seems more real to them, even if it is more complex and potentially confusing. Most children have little difficulty realizing when they are being talked down to, and they do not like it. They often prefer to work with adult material, learn what they can from it, and not worry about the rest.

--The goal of studying is often assumed to be getting the right answer; a student who does not know an answer is criticized. An alternative perspective is that asking stimulating questions is more important than knowing answers, especially since many questions do not have one commonly accepted right answer. In this view, it is all right not to know the answer to a question, even to a question with a clear "right answer." If a learner wants more information, he can look it up or ask someone.

--A mistake is often seen as a problem for which the learner needs to be punished with a low grade, ridicule, humiliation, etc. Some mistakes can be life-threatening, and children need warning and protection. But many mistakes provide learning opportunities and raw material for new discoveries. When children study something they value, they recognize and correct many of their own mistakes. If a sentence does not make sense, they go back to find the incorrect word. And children spending their own money understand the importance of getting the right answer. Also some so-called mistakes could be redefined. I remember watching a young ice skater glide a few times, fall, get up, glide, fall again. She was having a wonderful time, apparently did not feel she was making mistakes (at least they were not a problem to her), and I am sure she eventually learned to skate without falling.

--The need for pressure, in forms such as competition and testing, to keep children motivated is another common assumption. But some people feel that learning is its own reward, that children who are allowed to pursue their own interests and abilities are willing workers, that competition creates unnecessary tension, and that testing interferes with learning, partly because it is a vote of no confidence in the learner.

--That learning should be done in an orderly fashion, with each student sitting quietly in her place, is another assumption. In fact, many people learn better if they can move around while learning or at least at frequent intervals during the process, and some people even find they can accomplish something if they can move around that they simply cannot do while sitting still.

--Another common assumption is that adults, being larger and older, know more that children. But some people who have worked closely with children and observed them carefully realize that sometimes children know more than adults. Children, especially if they have been allowed to think and explore freely

31

and have not been subjected to the confines of conventional schools, can sometimes see things with a freshness and clarity that adults find very difficult to achieve. Children often see through hypocrisy, have fewer prejudices, and are more willing to trust their instincts and intuition. Fortunate indeed is the adult who has the opportunity to learn with a child.

This then is a sampler of some common assumptions about learning and alternatives to them. Ponder them, if you will, and add your own. Your assumptions inevitably influence your home school, and you may find it worthwhile to be aware of them.

ALTERNATIVE APPROACHES TO LEARNING

Home schooling parents need to decide how they will approach their family's learning. Several alternatives are described here. In reality the distinctions are somewhat artificial, since the alternatives overlap and often different types of learning go on simultaneously. But the distinctions are presented because they may clarify ideas about learning and because too often learner-led learning is not recognized as an acceptable way of learning.

--One approach could be called textbook learning. The student usually sits at a desk, reads what someone else says he should know, writes a few examples to practice applying what he has been told, and takes a test. This is not the most common, the most effective, the most efficient, the most exciting, or the most reliable way to learn. But it is the most widely recognized, the most visible, the most familiar, the most easily identified and tested, and the most easily controlled approach to learning. There are times when it can be an acceptable way to learn, such as when a learner wants to be exposed to a limited amount of material on a specific subject in a short time. It also has limitations: the learner has little choice about what she can learn (she can, of course, choose not to learn), and she has little, if any, experience with discovery and creative problem solving. Too much emphasis on this approach can interfere with other ways of learning.

--A related but broader and more flexible approach could be called conventional learning. The learner is told that there is a generally accepted body of information that many people have found useful (a typical school curriculum). The learner's job is to figure out what it is and learn it. A teacher is available to present much of the information and test him to see if he has learned it. There are advantages to this approach. For example, what the learner learns (or at least is exposed to) is roughly comparable to what others are learning. The learner receives guidance and direction in determining what to learn and in learning it (however, this may sometimes be inappropriate). There is a sense of completion on finishing the assignment, textbook, etc. The learner is at least exposed to a varied and well-rounded selection of information. Among the disadvantages are that the learner is limited in what he is exposed to and thus can learn, and the approach fosters dependence of the learner on the teacher and/or curriculum.

Both textbook and conventional learning are often used in connection with a purchased curriculum. Such a curriculum provides a definite structure, a clear starting point. It can make home schooling seem a lot less overwhelming and make it possible for some people to start home schooling who otherwise would not. (This book contains less discussion of purchased or prepared curriculums than of alternative approaches to learning; curriculums come with their own directions for use.)

--A third approach could be called "learner-led learning." It can be used as a family's main approach or it can be used along with or as a supplement to a conventional approach. Families using a purchased curriculum may find that including some learner-led learning adds new dimensions and ways of learning.

In leader-led learning, the learner plays a key role in determining what she will learn, how she will learn it, and when she is finished. Often learning is unplanned and seems to "just happen," as when a baby learns to walk and talk or when an adult learns from life experience. A guide may be available to provide support and assist in finding resources but is not necessary for

33

learning to occur. (However, in home schooling, a parent or parent substitute is needed to provide general guidance.) Potential advantages include the fact that the learner is usually motivated to learn, develops confidence in herself, and sees learning as a lifelong process. She learns how to learn and often remembers more than she would using a conventional approach, so learning is more efficient and less time is required for review. This approach gives the learner a chance to get to know herself as well as the subject and maximizes her abilities, talents, and strengths. One area of study usually leads to another, and the learner gets a more accurate picture of the world than she does working within the artificial confines and distinctions of a standardized curriculum. She is also more likely to make new discoveries. Among the possible disadvantages is the chance of gaps in the learner's basic knowledge. (This is probably less likely to occur than when a learner is forced to study something she is not ready for.) The fact that learner-led learning is not widely recognized as "real learning" means the learner and her family may be criticized for lack of an appropriate approach to education, especially since it is often difficult to record, document, or demonstrate this type of learning.

Another problem with learner-led learning is that it often goes unnoticed. It seems so natural, easy, and enjoyable that people do not stop to say, "That is learning." A home schooling parent who is concerned about whether his children are learning enough, or who is required to document for the state that learning is occurring, may want to learn to recognize at least some of the many ways in which children learn. We learn with our whole bodies, not just our brains. We learn with our hearts and our souls. Excellent insights are provided by John Holt's *How Children Learn* and *Learning All the Time* and Thomas Armstrong's *In Their Own Way*. (However, Armstrong places too much emphasis on the parent's identifying and encouraging a child's learning style. Actually, given an appropriate and supportive environment, a child will learn, without anyone's needing to worry about why or how.) A few of the ways children learn are:

--Through problem solving. Children can set a goal, try to achieve it, sometimes make mistakes, encounter problems along the way, and solve them.

--Through observing people and interacting with them. Home schoolers have the advantage of contact with a wide range of people of differing ages and backgrounds. They are not limited to spending school days with children their own age.

--Through being in the world of nature. Children observe closely, develop a sense of the order of things and the processes by which nature works.

--Through play. Whole books have been written about the value and importance of play. Among other things, children can invent a variety of situations and problems and figure out ways to handle them. They can learn to cooperate with other people.

--Through many other ways that readers may want to add here, based on their own learning experiences and observations of their children.

Additional insights into learning can also be gained by considering the difference between inductive and deductive approaches. In general terms, in inductive learning the learner applies a generalization he has been given to a set of specific examples, while deductive learning involves the learner's figuring out his own generalizations based on his observation of and experience with many examples. Conventional schools tend to emphasize inductive learning, but there are many strengths to deductive learning which allows the learner to make his own discoveries and draw his own conclusions. He is more likely to understand and remember.

It should not be assumed that when a home school is based on learner-led learning, the parent does nothing and the child does anything he pleases. The parent has serious and important responsibilities, a key role to play, and final authority in some areas. The difference in learner-led learning is that the learner has much more control over decisions about what he will learn, when, and how than does a learner in conventional learning. The amount of control the learner has varies with each individual situation, and within a given situation it changes over time as the parent feels he needs to exert some influence or the learner asserts independence. The process of arriving at and maintaining a balance is a fascinating one. In many ways the parent is the final authority, including in the eyes of society and the law, but in the final analysis, it is the learner who learns.

Does this mean that our children do not need us? That as home schooling parents we should do nothing, just stay out of their way and let them learn? Absolutely not. Our children need us desperately. But they do not need us to teach them, in the conventional sense of the word. They do not need us to make sure they learn all the right stuff. Among other things, they need us to

--keep them out of school for as long as this is the best
    alternative.
--protect them from the invasion of privacy and assault on
    thinking that is commonly called standardized testing.
--enable them to concentrate on learning and not have to
    worry about unannounced visits from school personnel.
--protect them from physical harm and help them stay healthy.
--protect them from intellectual harm from people who would
    put them down.
--have confidence in them when their own confidence falters.
--love them.

One of a home schooling parent's major responsibilities is to provide her child with a learning environment. Ideally it includes a variety of simple and inexpensive materials (arts and crafts supplies, books and other reference materials, writing supplies, etc.) and a pleasant space in which she can work freely. More important than supplies is an atmosphere that provides security, support, encouragement, freedom to explore, warmth, and love. The environment also includes a variety of interesting people, access to the out-of-doors, visits to interesting places, space for physical activity, etc. For more ideas about home schooling environments, see pp. 54-57.

Two parental activities can interfere with learner-led learning. One is testing, either as a formal written test or as informal questioning. ("Do you know what 17 times 39 is?" "Can you read this sentence?") Testing interferes with learning by disrupting its sequence and possibly making the learner come to a conclusion before she is ready. It is also a vote of no confidence in the learner. If a parent feels he really needs to know what a child has learned, he can simply observe her for a while and see for himself.

A second source of interference occurs when a parent decides to turn chance events into teaching opportunities by launching into an explanation or when a parent turns a question from a child into an exercise in "What do you think?" and "I will give you a hint." It is generally best to simply answer the question the child has asked, so he can use the information in whatever way he chooses and ask for more details if he wants them.

ALTERNATIVE APPROACHES TO TRADITIONAL SUBJECTS

These alternative approaches can be used with any subject. Actually that is misleading, because it is not so much a matter of applying these methods as recognizing when learning is occurring and realizing that there are many ways of learning besides sitting down with a book or being taught by someone. The ideas presented here are intended as suggestions to help you think about the range of choices so you can support your child as she explores approaches to learning. They are not definitive and they are not presented as things everyone should do. So take them in that spirit, use what makes sense to you, and add insights and discoveries from your own thinking and experience.

In reading these ideas, remember that the very process of dividing knowledge up into subjects is artificial, cumbersome, and often troublesome. The world is really one, the parts interrelated. If you look out the window, you see one scene, not architecture in the house next door, geology in the rocks, reading in the street sign. Subject divisions developed for convenience, especially of school people who try to contain and control knowledge. Home schoolers have the option of minimizing these divisions as much as possible. But the divisions are discussed here because they are so widespread and because home schoolers are sometimes forced to deal with them. For example, Wisconsin's home schooling law requires that home schoolers provide a "sequentially progressive curriculum...in reading, language arts, mathematics, social studies, science and health."

Also, some home schoolers rely on the maxim, "First, do no harm" when introducing a subject to their children. They realize that it is essentially impossible to get through a day without some exposure to all the basic subjects and also impossible to study only one subject without getting involved in others as well. Therefore, they provide a child with a reasonable exposure to a subject-- maybe a colorful botany book from the library, better yet a look at a variety of plants on a walk or contact with someone who is interested in botany (not necessarily a botany teacher or trained botanist; a gardener or someone with a mild interest is fine). If the child shows no particular interest, and especially if the child resists, these parents drop the subject immediately, feeling that it is far better for the child to continue without any additional information about botany, at least for the time being, than to have a negative experience and become convinced that she "does not like botany" or "is no good at botany," ideas that will then have to be overcome before much more intentional learning about botany occurs. But these parents also feel that there is much more knowledge available than anyone could ever learn, remember, and use. Maybe botany will be one thing this child does not learn much about. It is an exciting subject, but skipping it is all right, too. One does not need to study botany to eat broccoli. And if this child has a real predisposition toward botany, she will undoubtedly discover it herself, sooner or later. In other words, many home schooling parents feel it is very important to expose their child to a range of subjects, or more accurately, to as much of the world as possible, but it is equally important for parents to respect their child's interests and not pressure her. "First, do no harm."

(1) READING

Ideally a child will learn to read in such a way that he will want to read throughout his life. (Functionally there is no difference between a person who cannot read and one who knows how to read but does not.) A variety of programs are available for parents who want to teach their children to read. Another alternative is to let a child figure out how to read on her own, providing encouragement, support, and if she asks for it, assistance. Many parents provide an environment that encourages a child to learn to read, which may include the following:

--Lots of print, including books that mean something to the child, books that are important to other people, notes and letters addressed to the child, maps, posters, shopping lists, catalogs, etc. (Do not assume that a child who is not reading books regularly cannot read.)

--People who read themselves and talk about it.

--People who will respond to a child's questions by simply telling him what a word or sentence says. Many parents find it works best not to ask a child to sound out a word, correct what he reads, or try to explain phonics, unless the child wants these. Reading tests, even informal ones ("Do you know what that sign says?"), interfere with a child's learning process and are basically a vote of no confidence. Parents who are concerned about their child's reading abilities can simply observe the reading he does voluntarily, aloud or to himself. "First, do no harm."

--Sounds of reading. The language of books sounds different from everyday speech. To be able to make sense of books she is trying to read, a child needs to be exposed to the language of books. Reading aloud also shows a child that books are worth reading. Many parents enjoy these shared family times as much as the kids do. It is worth some effort to find good books through recommendations from friends, books such as Beverly Kobrin's *Eyeopeners!* (non-fiction) and Jim Trelease's *Read-Aloud Handbook* (mostly fiction), mail order catalogs, etc. Let the reader choose a style he likes, whether very dramatic or straightforward. Some listeners like to cuddle, others to move around, evidence of differences in learning styles. Make the reading suit your purposes: read the end of a book first if you want, skip unappealing parts, criticize or abandon a book you do not like, do not limit your reading to "children's books," reread favorite passages or whole books. Continue reading aloud even after your children can read themselves. For a long time children can think about material that is much more complicated than what they can read themselves.

--Prerecorded audio tapes make reading aloud easy, although they are not as warm and friendly as a "real" person reading.

--Access to writing. Reading and writing go hand in hand. A child should see other people writing and have a chance to try writing herself, even before she can read.

--Carefully selected television or none at all. It interferes with reading.

But what if, despite a supportive environment, an older child has not learned to read? Does a parent need to do something more to prevent lifelong illiteracy?

--First, find out how your child is feeling. If he feels inadequate or is losing self-esteem and self-confidence because he is not reading as well as he wants to, it is time to do something. You could discuss the situation with him, share some of the information below, and see if he is comfortable waiting a little longer. Or you could try some of the suggestions below.

--If the pressure is coming from within yourself or from other people, ask whether it is necessary to worry or whether you can wait to see if she learns on her own. Remember that learning to read is a lifelong process. There is no clear point at which a child officially knows how to read, and ideally an adult can read better now than he could five years ago. Remember that generally the physiological developments necessary to be able to read occur later in boys than in girls. In fact, if there were separate reading levels for boys and girls, many "late reading problems" would be defined out of existence. The problem is not that some children, especially boys, read "late." Rather too many children are forced to learn to read too early, before they are really ready. (Note that because of normal differences in children, some want to and can read at an early age, say 4 or 5. This is one of their strengths and talents and is fine for them. It just should not be required of children who are gifted in other areas.) Many children have learned to read well and enthusiastically beginning when they were 9, or 12, or older. Reading ability does not improve at a constant rate; many late readers catch up with their contemporaries in a year or two.

--Keep reading in perspective. Reading can bring a wealth of information and enjoyment, enhance understanding and communication, etc., etc. (Authors have to be committed to literacy, and you, the reader, obviously know the value of reading, so we do not need to discuss this point further.) But there are many other ways to learn, some of them more exciting, valuable, and rewarding. Reading has so much significance in our culture partly because schools (which are isolated, sterile, and removed from the real world) find it convenient and necessary to base most teaching on reading and writing.

--There are advantages to being a person who does not read. Such a child has the time, energy, and incentive to explore other approaches to learning. He is not distracted by print. He may have a better memory than a reader who knows subconsciously that she can refer to printed matter. Parents of older children who do not read have an opportunity to learn about alternatives in learning.

41

--If you really feel you must do something further to help your child learn to read, here are some suggestions:

(1) Continue to read aloud to your child. The goal is to have her regard reading as a positive, enjoyable experience.

(2) You could have his vision checked, although Frank Smith says in *Reading Without Nonsense* (p. 9) that a child who can tell the difference between a pin and a paper clip on the table in front of him has the visual acuity necessary to read. (This does not mean he should be reading, only that visual problems are not preventing him.) Information on working with a child with visual problems is in Lori and Bill Granger's *Magic Feather*.

(3) Work only with material that makes sense to the child and appeals to her. According to Frank Smith in *Reading Without Nonsense*, readers recognize words and understand their meaning from the context in which they occur, so if the context is not appropriate, reading is much more difficult for a child. Children's response to easy readers varies; some find them objectionable and insulting. Do not assume that easy readers will be right for your child just because they are widely heralded as improvements over Dick and Jane. Some beginning readers prefer books by authors like Edward W. and Marguerite P. Dolch, Laura Ingalls Wilder, or Gertrude Chandler Warner. It often works well to begin with one of the child's favorite books, one she knows well so that the reading is not too difficult even if it is on a higher "reading level."

(4) Encourage your child to sit next to someone who is reading aloud and look at the book while he listens to the words. (An audio tape can be used instead, but that is not as warm and friendly and may be more difficult to follow.) A marker held under the line being read may help.

(5) Suggest that your child read herself a familiar book. Then she can read the words she knows, skips the ones she does not recognize, and still follow the story. (Actually she will begin to recognize some of the unknown words from context.)

(6) Assure your child that he can simply skip many of the words he does not know. A reader can understand what he is reading without identifying every word, and good readers regularly skip words they do not know or guess at their meaning and proceed.

(7) A child can read aloud to an experienced reader who supplies pronunciations for words the child does not recognize. Try this with caution--it is much more difficult to read aloud than to read silently. A better approach for some children is to sit next to an experienced reader, read silently, and have the experienced reader identify needed words. And of course there is the spell-the-word-aloud-to-Mom-who-is-in-the-kitchen-cooking-dinner approach, without which many people might not have learned to read. This is fine if Mom can recognize oral spellings out of context without burning the beans. Whichever of these variations is used, the experienced reader should simply supply the requested word--no hints, no sound-it-outs, no "You recognized that word in line before this." The goal is to help the child learn to read, not to confuse, frustrate, or humiliate her.

(8) Do not worry if your child recognizes a word once, or even three times, and then is stumped the next time he sees it. This is a normal part of learning to read and stops eventually.

(9) Encourage your child to learn to juggle or walk on stilts. This may encourage the development of connections between the right and left halves of his brain, a fact which is included here only so you will take the suggestion seriously--it really does not matter why it works. Activities like jigsaw puzzles and origami foster development of shape recognition, etc. In addition to helping your child, these activities enable you to say honestly to a school official or a concerned friend (or to yourself and your child) that she is working on reading and making progress.

(10) A good basic phonics book such as Kathryn Diehl and G.K. Hodenfield's *Johnny STILL Can't Read--But You Can Teach Him at Home* may be helpful to you or your child, but remember that it

is much easier to learn phonics after you can recognize some words and begin to figure out phonics deductively.

(11) Realize that when people share stories about their older children learning to read and making amazing progress very quickly, they are talking about progress over a period of months and years. Daily progress is often slow, especially at first. Do not get discouraged. And keep reading aloud to your child, even as his ability increases.

A few random ideas on some other subjects:

SPELLING

Spelling is a useful communication tool. It is also a kind of credential which some people feel indicates that a person is educated (a questionable assumption). For this reason some home schoolers feel it is important that they learn to spell well. However, since perfect spelling requires a lot of effort for some people and is not essential to communication. (When was the last time you truly misunderstood something because of a misspelled word?) Therefore, many parents encourage their children to develop a general sense of how English is spelled and not worry about an occasional "-ance" which should have been "-ence." Dictionaries and spelling checks in computers can improve accuracy when correct spelling is desired. The important point is for each family to decide how essential spelling is and not just assume it is critical and then feel inadequate if they are not perfect spellers.

Many parents feel spelling is best absorbed through a child's experience with reading and writing. They encourage their child to begin writing with "invented spelling," his best guess at the spelling of the words he wants to write. The results are fascinating, generally improve dramatically in a fairly short time, and are surprisingly easy to read. Another advantage of home schooling is that parents can read more of their children's invented spelling than could someone who knew them less well; thus parents can encourage beginning writers and spellers. It is certainly unfortunate when a child misses the joy of writing because he thinks he cannot spell well enough. Children who want to work on spelling can make flash cards for words they select with the correct spelling on one side and a picture, definition, or sentence with the word missing on the other side. Then they can test themselves, if they choose.

MATH

Getting a feel for the way numbers work is more important than memorizing multiplication tables and other math facts, according to many parents. Memorizing rules can interfere with a child's developing number sense. As with reading, much math can be learned from daily living as a child spends her allowance, balances the family checkbook, etc. Many books of math games, puzzles, and history are available for people who want exposure to more complicated math than daily life naturally provides but do not want to study confusing rules.

SOCIAL STUDIES

Studying social studies includes realizing that in order to survive, a group of people living together have to work out a way of organizing themselves and getting along. There are many different ways in which this can be and has been done. Also, one can develop a sense of history, understanding that things are the way they are because of what has happened before. Meeting people from other cultures, eating ethnic foods, reading about other times and places help make these ideas concrete and real. Locating places on a map or globe as you hear about them will help your child learn a lot of geography meaningfully and painlessly. Many home schoolers have significant direct personal experience with government as a result of battles against unreasonable regulation of home schools.

ARTS AND CRAFTS

Arts and crafts provide excellent opportunities for hands-on learning, creative thinking, problem solving, building self-esteem as well as being fun and empowering as one builds competence. Mona Brooks' *Drawing With Children* is great for parents and children who want to learn to draw but think they are no good at it.

CONCLUSION

It is exciting to explore the many ways in which people learn and the variety of material which can be studied. But to be able to take advantage of this wealth of opportunity, to allow our children as many alternative approaches to learning as possible, to have home schooling be the true alternative it should be, home schoolers must be free from unnecessary regulation. This means we must be politically active and take responsibility for regaining and maintaining our rights. We owe it to our children to enable them to continue home schooling without undue regulation and interference. For ideas about how this can be done, see Parts III, IV, and V of this book.

CHAPTER 5

EVALUATING LEARNING AND KEEPING RECORDS

EVALUATING THE LEARNING OF HOME SCHOOLING CHILDREN

Non-home schoolers sometimes contend that the learning of home schooled children should be evaluated by means of standardized testing, review by a public school official, or some other method in order to be sure that the children are learning what they need to know. However, home schooling parents do a good job of evaluating their children's learning without the state's requiring evaluation. Among the ways this may be done:

--Parents naturally and automatically observe and evaluate their children, without needing to plan or think about it, because they like their children, are interested in what they say and do, and want them to get the best possible education. Parents then make adjustments as a result of these observations. They do extra reading with a child who is having trouble decoding words. Special notes are written to a child who needs encouragement with writing. The cost of new clothes or toys is discussed with a child who does not like math. Parents do these things because they care about their children and want to help them learn.

--Many parents also make deliberate and self-conscious observations of their children. These observations are guided by the family's plans and goals. Parents ask themselves questions like: What interests my child? What skills has she mastered or made progress on? What does she do with free time? What kinds of questions does she ask? (Perhaps the real measure of intelligence is not the ability to answer questions but the ability to ask them.)

--Some parents ask their child how he feels about what he has learned, if there are other things he feels he should have learned, if some things that he wants to learn seem too hard to learn, and if there are other things he would be interested in learning. These parents do not give up their responsibility for their home schooling program and just let their child do anything he wants, but they do give serious consideration to their child's interests and desires.

--Evaluating a child's learning environment can also be helpful. Many parents ask themselves what more they could do to encourage learning. Does the child have a variety of things to look at, listen to, and work with? Are there enough reference books with information that interests the child? Maps on the wall? Are there other learning aids that would be intriguing to the child? Many parents find that some of the best learning aids are the tools and materials that adults use to do their work. Many children have learned by using their parents' computer, sewing machine, wood working equipment, garden tools, etc.

--Many parents also find it helpful to review their home school records (see below) to evaluate learning. It is helpful to compare what a child was able to do in the past with his present abilities. Home schooling parents thus can assess what a child has learned so far and what he still needs to work on.

--Some home schooling parents simply accept the limits on what they can know about their child's learning. They observe major things such as whether their child can read and has a general sense of how numbers work together. They are alert for clues about what their child might like to learn or feels she needs to learn. They offer support, encouragement, materials, and guidance. But they do not worry about the exact details of what their child knows. Seeing that she enjoys reading and is choosing increasingly complex books, they do not worry about what reading level she is on. (In fact, some feel reading levels are just another artificial construct of conventional schools--some books have more complicated words, but basically each book exists on several levels and people read it on a variety of levels.) These parents feel it is important that their child be able to learn in ways that are appropriate to her interests and abilities; that she know how to ask questions, gather resources, and begin investigating a specific topic she has chosen; and that she find value and satisfaction in this process. But they also feel that what she specifically knows is her business, and they do not want to invade her privacy or take the responsibility for learning away from her. In a real sense, no one can know what another person knows; in some ways, the person herself may not be really aware of all she knows. And that is just fine. These parents feel that imposing unwanted tests or other forms of evaluation on their child is a violation of the child and destroys something fragile and beautiful that is just unfolding, like prying open a flower bud or tearing down a spider's web. They provide their child with love, support, and a chance to explore the world, and instead of worrying about what she is learning, they try to keep the state from imposing regulations that would interfere with her learning.

RECORD KEEPING

Home schoolers keep records for a variety of reasons. Records help parents evaluate progress toward goals and contribute to a child's sense of accomplishment and self-esteem. They contribute to the achievement of goals; recording something when it is completed gives extra motivation to get it done. Records are also invaluable if a family's compliance with a home schooling law is questioned or challenged.

One of the most important parts of record keeping is learning to recognize the many ways in which children learn. Doing a page of subtraction problems is obviously math, but so is figuring out what you can afford to buy and making sure you get the correct change. Reading a textbook on Japan is obviously social studies, but so is listening to grandpa talk about his boyhood on the farm. (For more ideas on alternative ways of learning, see pp. 27-46.)

Valuable as records may be, they need to be kept in perspective. It does not make sense to spend so much time keeping records that there is not enough time for activities a family wants to do. Also, home schooling should not be abandoned just because record keeping seems overwhelming. If one approach to record keeping does not work well, another can be tried. Older children can keep some of their own records.

Some families keep two sets of records, a daily attendance record and a more detailed journal or log. If they are contacted by a truant officer, they can use the attendance record to document that their child is not truant without having to show their more complex and personal set of records. (For more information on responding to contact from school officials, see pp. 249-256.)

At the beginning of the school year, some home schoolers establish a calendar that complies with requirements of their state law and draw up a chart. For example:

	Aug.					Sept.				
	26	27	28	29	30	2	3	4	5	6
Johnny	P	P	P	P	P	H	P	P	P	P
Mary	P	P	P	P	P	H	P	P	P	P
Fred	P	P	P	P	P	H	P	P	P	P

P = present, A = absent, S = sick, H = holiday

There are a variety of ways a more detailed set of records can be kept.

--Some families write a plan of activities they intend to do during the next day or week. As activities are completed, the time spent on each is noted along with comments, if desired, and the plan becomes a record. Unplanned activities are added to complete the record.

--Some parents choose a narrative style, essentially writing a journal. This can include all kinds of interesting comments. If it is intended to document compliance with a legal requirement that a home school operate for a given number of hours or days, this figure needs to be included.

--Some parents like to write periodic reports, pausing once every month, or three months, or whenever, to review and evaluate the learning that is taking place.

--A portfolio with samples of a child's work can be satisfying to the child as well as to interested adults. It should include more than paperwork--either write a description, include a child's drawing, or take a photograph of accomplishments like cooking dinner, raising an animal, producing a play, or building an elaborate block structure. This record may not be as complete as others described above, unless it includes a listing of daily activities and hours spent.

CHAPTER 6

STRENGTHENING YOUR HOME SCHOOL

Eager to provide their children with the best education possible, home schooling parents strive to make their home school as strong as possible. They may find it helpful to ask themselves questions such as: Are we making the best use of available space, or should we reorganize parts of the house? Are we using resources in our community well? How are we dealing with problems and frustrations? Ideas about these and other questions are presented in this chapter. Please remember that these are suggestions only; each family must make its own decisions.

THE IMPORTANCE OF LISTENING TO YOUR CHILD

Many parents find that listening to their child is one of the most important things they do. It provides clues and insights into how he thinks, what interests him, what he has learned, what his concerns are, etc. It helps parents figure out how to help their child learn. The idea of listening to a child sounds logical, ordinary, and easy, but it is not. We live in a society which seldom trusts children or treats them with respect. The idea that adults know more than children and should make their decisions for them, according to the needs and convenience of the adults, may be more deeply ingrained in us than we realize or wish. In addition, considerable effort is required to listen actively, to hear what someone wants to say, not what the listener wants or expects to hear, and to respond. The listener has to set aside his preconceived ideas and concerns, have an open mind, consider what the speaker is really saying in addition to the literal meaning of his words, and respond emotionally as well as intellectually-- not an easy task but definitely worthwhile.

Many parents find it works well to begin listening seriously when their child is a baby, but it is never too late to decide to listen more. Sometimes a good response to what a child says is a question. "How do you feel about the picture you just drew?" "Why do you think your foot hurts?" "What do you want to do about the broken airplane?" "How do you feel about what she said?" "Do you want to go to his house?" (These questions are a way of asking the child what she thinks or feels; they are very different from informal testing such as "Do you know the capital of France?") Information from questions such as these can keep us from wasting time and working at cross purposes, but more is involved than that. These questions help parents take their child seriously as a person, and they help the child learn to think for herself, make decisions, and gain confidence in what she can handle. Of course this does not mean that the parents always or automatically do what the child wants. But it does mean that they have much better information on which to base their decisions.

PRACTICAL IDEAS ABOUT LEARNING

Many parents discover that their home school improves when they decide to learn something new themselves and work on it. They set a good example for their child, of course, but they also gain insights into the learning process when they ask themselves: What helped me the most? What interfered with my learning? If the project was short-term and clearly defined, how did I feel when I completed it? How would I have felt if someone had given me a test either while I was in the process of learning or after I had finished?

Home schooling often goes more smoothly when parents give their child as much responsibility for her own learning as possible. After all, she is the one who has to do the work involved in learning and who will benefit from it. When learning is seen as the parents' responsibility, the child may try to learn in order to please her parents or may refuse to learn in order to upset them. When it is seen as the child's responsibility, she is free to focus on learning for its own sake, and her parents can focus on supporting her work rather than trying to get her to study. This encourages independent study and lifelong learning.

Many children learn more willingly, more easily, more quickly, and more permanently from real experiences than from books. Of course books can be very helpful and are sometimes essential--one cannot visit ancient Greece. Sometimes learning from books is quicker and more convenient. But it is exciting to discover something oneself, and things learned from experience are often understood more clearly and remembered longer. This does not mean that parents have to decide what their child should know and then devise practical experiences that will enable him to discover it. This works sometimes, as in some exercises with math manipulatives and science experiments. But more often the child simply discovers something interesting about the world that is readily available around him. Parents can encourage learning by making as much of the world accessible to their child as possible and providing guidance and protection, if needed, while he explores it.

PROVIDING A SUPPORTIVE LEARNING ENVIRONMENT

Many parents find that putting time and thought into setting up a supportive learning environment (in other words, organizing the house) helps their child learn through interaction with his environment. It allows the child to work at his own pace and saves the parents time and energy. Such an environment need not be expensive; it requires more ingenuity than money.

Homes of home schoolers may look different from those which are empty between 7 AM and 5 PM. The variety and amount of activity that occurs in a home school may be apparent; it may serve as a learning center, gym, craft center, science lab, music studio, computer center, and library as well as a home. Conventional rooms may have unconventional equipment and resources in them: encyclopedias in the dining room, desks in the kitchen. Many home schooling parents find that the more relaxed and flexible they can be about the appearance and use of the house, while maintaining reasonable standards of cleanliness and order, the more learning occurs.

Many parents structure their learning environments to encourage a wide range of learning styles (such as those described in Thomas Armstrong's *In Their Own Way*). They ask what their family needs the environment to provide. Among the possibilities:

--Easy access to basic supplies (paper, pencils, etc.), to reference materials (encyclopedias, globes, maps, posters, books, etc.), and to tools, equipment and supplies for repair work, sewing, cooking, writing, typing, etc. Ideally everything has its place, and everyone puts things away when finished with them. This works in some families that are well organized. But others find that while they are waiting for everyone to learn this (some parents are notorious for taking longest), it is easier and less stressful simply to buy multiples of key tools, such as scissors and staplers, to increase the chances of being able to find one.

--User-friendly, sturdy, easily cleaned work areas; lots of flat surfaces like desks and tables are especially valuable.

--Quiet areas and places where it is all right to make noise and/or different times for quiet and noise. Hearing protectors worn by people who work near jet planes can reduce noise for one person, head phones and ear plugs allow for individualized listening, and an extension phone in a separate room can eliminate both background noise that distracts the person using the phone and the disruption of an overheard phone conversation.

55

--A balance between order and the stimulation that comes from having materials and works in progress clearly visible. If members of the family vary in their need for order, an agreement may be made to keep some parts of the house more orderly than others.

--A separate space for each person. A room of one's own has advantages but is not necessary; space can be divided in a mutually acceptable way and shared. Many children like to have an area of their own (a desk, cupboard, etc.) within the family living area, even if they have their own room, so they can work near others or along with them.

--Many families find that more important than the shape and organization of the physical environment is the attitude of the people who live in it. Each person's privacy (expressed in diaries, letters, etc.) and personal belongings are protected and respected. Appropriate space is available for children to experiment, paint, etc. without being criticized for making a mess. Ideas and new things can be tried and mistakes made without fear of embarrassment or ridicule. Varying degrees of commitment to order and neatness are accepted by all.

It may be helpful to consider some of the following questions:

--Do we have any unused or seldom used space that could be put into service? Can bedrooms be used during the day? Can the dining room be used for other activities? It helps to be willing to be unconventional; turn a pantry into a child's private space, set up the computer in the dining room.

--Can children study in or near parents' work areas so parents can answer questions and provide support? Desks in the kitchen are an example.

--Should we reorganize our house now that family members have grown and interests have changed? Do our most pressing current interests have priority for the best space? Do the most readily available storage areas house the most frequently used items?

USING THE PUBLIC LIBRARY AND OTHER COMMUNITY RESOURCES

It is definitely worth the effort to develop a good working relationship with the people who work in your local library; they can be an invaluable asset. Take time to find out what services they can provide, how you can make their job easier, and what format you should use in requesting books, tapes, and other materials. Ask how you can get materials from regional, state, and national interlibrary loan systems. If you make many requests, work out a form that is easy for the librarians to work from and consider establishing a regular day each week to pick up your materials, so the librarians do not have to call you each time a book arrives. Think of ways to show your appreciation and support the library, such as volunteering to read shelves or do other work (the whole family can be involved), joining the Friends of the Library (or organizing such a group yourself), running a used book sale, or donating money. In addition to all the free resources you will receive from the library, a librarian with whom you have worked closely can be a valuable ally and reference if someone begins questioning the competence or acceptability of your home school.

Use of other community resources is determined by what is available and your family's interests. Many children benefit from interacting with adults and not being limited to children's programs, activities, and organizations. An "adult level" presentation on birds or quilting is often more interesting and satisfying than a children's program that is oversimplified and condescending, and it does not seem to bother many children if parts of the presentation are over their heads. If the resources they want are not available, home schoolers may start new organizations, centers, programs, etc.

SOLVING PROBLEMS

Home schooling works well and is really exciting. However, sometimes home schools do not run smoothly. Conscientious parents sometimes worry, question what they are doing, and feel discouraged. Here are some observations that may be helpful.

Many parents put home schooling "problems" in perspective by looking carefully at the size and cause of them. Was it really a bad day, a whole day? Was it not actually a difficult 15 minutes, or maybe two challenging half hours? Should a whole day be labeled and sacrificed because one or two things went wrong? How much difference will these "catastrophes" make an hour from now? By tomorrow? In a week? A month? By any chance do they have a funny side that could be laughed about now?

Is this actually a home schooling problem? Is the real problem perhaps worries about money, or a serious illness, or difficulties with a parent's job, or rude comments a neighbor keeps making? Pressure and stress that have nothing to do with home schooling can create tensions that interfere with learning, but these are not home schooling problems. Some that could be called home schooling problems are:

IT SEEMS AS IF NO ONE IS LEARNING.

To whom have you been listening? Comparisons can be dangerous. Of course they are tempting and may even seem necessary. After all, we undertook a tremendous responsibility when we decided to home school. Do we not need comparisons so we know if we are on the right track, if our children are doing all right? To be sure, some kind of reassurance is helpful. Unfortunately we cannot get it from comparisons. Each one of us, whether parent or child, is unique. There has never been another person just like any one of us, so each of us has to determine what we are supposed to be doing. We cannot compare ourselves to other home schoolers and try to become like them, because we are all different. Of course there are some basic similarities, and we can learn from and be inspired by others, but home schooling on the basis of comparisons just does not work.

Another problem with comparisons among home schoolers is that we tend to combine things inappropriately. We listen to other parents and conclude we should be learning fractions the way the Smiths are, and studying astronomy like the Joneses, and working on Spanish like the Browns, and playing music like the Greens. We forget that even if it made sense for us to try to follow the example of one of these families in one of these activities, it would be way too much for us to try to do them all. Each of these families is not doing all of the things the other families are doing. We should concentrate on deciding what would be best for us to be doing.

Okay, okay, but what can we do on those dark days when it still seems as if no one is learning anything? This can be a good time to pull out the records we have been keeping (see p. 49 for suggestions) and consider what we were doing and how we were doing it a month ago, six months ago, a year ago, or even farther back. We can remember what it was like before we started home schooling. It becomes clear that everybody (parents included) has learned a lot recently--maybe not this morning or last week, but over the last six months or year.

Home schoolers who have not been keeping these kinds of records can gain perspective by remembering what their children were doing at some time in the past. "What were they doing last summer? Why, that was before John had even started all those chemistry experiments. And Mary was just learning to multiply-- look how well she's doing now." This kind of remembering can provide helpful perspective.

In a review like this, many home schoolers find it helpful to remember that children learn all kinds of things in all kinds of ways. It is not just a question of whether John has memorized multiplication tables; is he developing a sense of the way numbers work together and how he can use them in other projects? Many parents also find it helpful to review their non-academic goals and the progress their children are making in these areas, which may be more important, anyway. One can learn the basic operations of arithmetic with a fairly short period of concentrated work (if one is ready and motivated). But spiritual and moral values, ways of getting along with other people, and social responsibility cannot be learned this way--they are the result of years of thinking and doing.

MY CHILD IS HAVING TROUBLE WITH READING (OR MATH OR WHATEVER).

Learning is exciting and satisfying, but it is also hard work. Everyone has some trouble, each time he tries to learn something. But having difficulty does not mean one has a disability. It helps to be patient and not panic. Many parents find it also helps to ask the child what he thinks the problem is and what he would like to do about it. The reason for these questions is not to let the child do anything he pleases but rather to get the child's point of view and gain more insight into what the problem is and how it might be solved. Sometimes what seems like a difficult problem has a surprisingly simple solution, one that perhaps the parent had not thought of.

There are alternative ways of handling difficulties while learning, such as the following.

--Try a different approach. Written material that is incomprehensible when you are trying to read it silently can become much clearer if someone else reads it to you, even if you are an experienced reader. A change from looking at words to listening to them can give a whole new perspective. Or if you are having trouble with cursive, maybe learning to type or write on a word processor would be a better alternative.

--Change to a different book on the same subject. The new perspective from a different approach or explanation may clarify the material. Some duplication is all right; material that has already been learned from one book will be reinforced if it is covered by a second. Some families select individual books from different curriculums to get the benefits of a variety of approaches.

--Direct hands-on experiences provide learning opportunities not available through books. Math manipulatives such as blocks or rods make math facts concrete and real in a way that work sheets do not. A meal in an ethnic restaurant can help another culture come alive. Zoos and museums are well recognized for their educational value, but a great deal about nature can be learned from close observations in a back yard or nearby park. Balancing the family checkbook demonstrates the importance of learning math, as well as teaching a valuable skill.

--Set aside the material causing difficulty for a while. Things may go more smoothly with a fresh start after a break, or the material may be more manageable when the child is a little older. A child having trouble with fractions could work on percents or graphs instead. Or go a step further and set aside a whole subject area, like math, for a while and concentrate on other subjects, like reading and social studies. Or sometimes the problem may resolve itself. Many children have found that their spelling improved greatly when they stopped trying to memorize word lists and instead concentrated on reading widely and writing with invented spelling.

MY CHILD WILL NOT SETTLE DOWN AND STUDY.

Some parents find it helps to ask the child how she is feeling and why. What specifically does she object to? Would studying be easier if she had a different time or place to work? The reason for asking these questions is not to let the child do anything she pleases but rather to discover more about the problem and possible solutions. A different approach to one or more subjects, such as the alternatives described above, may be helpful.

Some parents feel the main goal is to help their child learn how to learn and start on a path of lifelong learning. They reason that it is more important that their child generally enjoy learning than that he learn to read or add or locate Spain today, or this week. Many learning opportunities are provided by helping a child discover and pursue activities he enjoys, whether these be arts and crafts projects, wood working, gardening, visiting an elderly neighbor, raising an animal, etc. Desire to find out more about a special interest has led many a formerly reluctant student into scholastic pursuits.

Sometimes a break helps. Among other things, it may allow a child to discover new interests that lead her back to studying in a new way or at least with less resistance.

THE KIDS SEEM TO SQUABBLE SO MUCH.

Having one or more siblings provides many learning opportunities along with opportunities for conflict. Many parents feel that on balance siblings do each other more good than harm; these parents try to take in stride a reasonable amount of squabbling.

It often helps to make sure everyone has a place of his own. A whole room is great, but many children manage well with a clearly marked part of a shared bedroom or even with just a corner or desk somewhere. What is important is that each child's privacy and possessions be respected by everyone in the family.

If a parent or someone else compares one sibling to another in a negative way, this can contribute to an antagonistic atmosphere. No one likes to hear, "Why is your brother so much neater than you are?" Instead, a parent who values the uniqueness of each child encourages siblings to accept each other and get along. It may also help to point out that learning is available to everyone. No need to get upset because Mary just learned to multiply--her learning does not in any way diminish John's chance to learn this, too.

Sometimes siblings squabble because they are bored and cannot think of anything better to do. Parents try to see that each child has enough opportunity to do things that interest him. Some families develop a repertoire of relaxing activities for times when tensions start building. Reading aloud, listening to music, or going for a walk are ways of encouraging siblings to do something constructive together.

THE KIDS RESIST HELPING WITH THE HOUSEWORK.

Some families begin by making sure that all the work on their "to do" list really needs to be done. They ask if there are any jobs that could be reduced or eliminated; kids often have ideas about this! When possible, they involve the kids in the process of selecting and planning the work. It helps if the kids understand why the work is important and why their participation is needed. Explanations can be general or specific (such as, if the child does not help, the parent will not have time to help him with his project). Some families try, as far as possible, to let people choose their own jobs. Parents help each child figure out how he works best. Some prefer to be responsible for a regular job, others would rather be called on as needed or change jobs frequently. Often it is easier to work if others are working at the same time, so some families have regular work times.

Some parents do the children's jobs themselves occasionally to see how it really feels to do each job, what parts of it are most tiresome or offensive, and how much it is appreciated. Some parents also help their children learn to identify what they do not like about a job and figure out if anything can be done to change this.

Keeping long-range goals in mind helps some families. They try to help kids see work as a worthwhile endeavor with many rewards. Work is not distinguished from play in some cultures which think in terms of activities. Family work can be organized so those most able to work at any given time do what needs to be done while those who have other concerns or commitments or demands on their time or are not feeling well are excused from work for that time.

Payment for work done is a great motivator in the short term but may interfere with a long-range goal of having family members help willingly because they are needed. It may also send the wrong signal about why one should work. Some families expect everyone to work and give regular allowances independent of work done.

FRIENDS, RELATIVES, AND NEIGHBORS SOMETIMES CRITICIZE MY HOME SCHOOL.

Support from neighbors, friends, and relatives is wonderful, and criticism can be especially frustrating to parents who have assumed a serious responsibility and are putting a lot of time and energy into their child's education. However, many families have happily and successfully home schooled with little or no support and in spite of much criticism. They often begin by deciding that it is more important to choose the approach to education that they feel is best for their child than to please others and win their approval. They realize that a person can be a good neighbor, friend or relative and still disagree with home schooling. They avoid antagonizing people unnecessarily. They make statements like, "Home schooling is working well for our family, but every family has to make its own decisions about education." They avoid comments like, "If you really cared about your child, you would be home schooling, too." They do not attack conventional schools.

When their home school is criticized, many parents listen carefully to try to understand the critic's real objections. Generally, critics fall into three groups. Some are open-minded enough to listen to information about home schooling and possibly change their minds once they understand it better. In this case, a home schooler may want to share personal experiences, ideas, and articles and books about home schooling. It often helps to explain that children learn in many different ways and also to use conventional school terms. For example, interlocking building blocks can be "math manipulatives" and learning to cook can be "home economics."

A second group of critics have their minds definitely made up and are simply not interested in learning more about home schooling. However, sometimes these people are willing to agree to disagree. They will continue their approach to education and will accept a home schooler's decision to home school. This approach avoids a lot of pointless discussion and makes it possible to continue a relationship on relatively good terms.

Unfortunately there is a third group of people who seem unable to accept the idea of home schooling. Some home schoolers find that they just have to give up, ask the person to stop talking about home schooling, and possibly stop seeing the person if she refuses. Having a relationship end this way can be sad and frustrating, but sometimes it seems the only choice. Many parents feel strongly about protecting their children from undue criticism, teasing, ridicule, or negative comments. Sometimes this means that the parent has to speak very firmly to a critic and possibly limit the child's contact with her.

AS A HOME SCHOOLING MOTHER (OR FATHER), I DO NOT HAVE ENOUGH TIME FOR MYSELF.

Finding enough time for everything that needs to be done is a problem that perplexes most home schoolers, and sometimes it seems as if mother's time for herself is what gets sacrificed first. Here are ways some mothers deal with this.

--Begin with realistic expectations. Home schooling does take a lot of time and energy. Some mothers find that if they expect to be interrupted while they are doing something on their own, they are less likely to be surprised or annoyed by an interruption and more able to deal with it and resume their activity.

--Some mothers include plans for their own learning when they are planning their child's curriculum. They may study some of the same topics their child is studying but on a more advanced level, such as reviewing American history or learning Spanish. Or they may pursue their own interest while the child studies independently nearby. Some families have a regular time when each person reads silently; mother can read what she chooses. Some mothers also find that they enjoy so much working with their child, exploring and learning new things themselves, that they count this as time for themselves as well as school time. A parent who is actively learning and enjoying it sets an outstanding example for her child.

--Sometimes what a mother needs is a change of pace, a break from daily routine. It may help to take a couple of hours to read a good book aloud, or go on a field trip, or share experiences and ideas with another home schooling family. Sometimes just a break from the house is a help. It is important to take time to do something for fun with a child. These are times when memories are made and family bonds forged.

--Sometimes it helps to see if there is anything else, not related to home schooling, that could be eliminated, so there would be more time for mother. Some people reduce the amount of time they watch TV, others begin saying "No" to unreasonable demands from people outside the immediate family, and others figure out ways to spend less time cleaning house while still meeting the necessary minimum standards of order and cleanliness.

--Perhaps the real problem is unrelated to home schooling, such as a serious illness or trouble with the neighbors. What a mother needs may be "time away from stress" rather than "time for herself." Resolving the problem is obviously the best solution but that may be impossible. An alternative is for a mother to make a deliberate and determined effort to set aside the difficulty, do something positive and pleasant with her child, and not worry for several hours or longer if possible.

--Some mothers consider the alternative. Having a child in school takes a lot of time and energy, too, and a parent has much less control over the whole situation, the results of which may be far less satisfactory than home schooling. The peace of mind that comes from knowing one is giving one's child a very important opportunity to learn at home keeps a lot of mothers going even when they have very little time for themselves.

SOLVING YOUR FAMILY'S PROBLEMS

The basic point of all this is that you are the one who has to solve your family's problems. No one else can do it for you. Your problems are unique. You have the best understanding of what the real problems are and what resources you have. The best solutions to whatever problems you are facing often grow out of the fabric of your own family, the unique strengths, abilities, and talents of each member. Some families seem to intuit this and solve problems without actually concentrating on them. Others find it helpful to have a model and step by step suggestions for doing this. Here is one possible model. A parent can use it by himself, but it is even better if you include other people who are involved with the problem.

(1) Identify the problem. Write it down. This is very important and may be harder than you expect. Sometimes we walk around assuming one thing is the problem, but when we actually sit down and think, it turns out to be something else.

(2) Think of as many possible solutions as you can. Write down lots of alternatives. See how many ideas you can come up with. This is not the time to decide whether something will work. Do not let any obstacles stand in your way. No fair saying, "But we cannot...." or "But we do not have any..."

(3) Review the alternatives and cross out the ones that are unacceptable or impossible. If more than one person is involved, listen to everyone.

(4) Decide what solution will work best and figure out specifically how it will be done. Everybody must agree, and it is best to have the agreement in writing.

(5) After a reasonable time, review the situation. Was the problem correctly identified? Is the solution working? If not, what should be tried?

Remember that problems provide opportunities to learn and grow. They give us strong incentive and get us going on things we might not get around to doing if it were not for the problem. Some of these things are too important to be missed. If this sounds too unrealistically positive, think about the most important things you have learned. How many of them were learned in response to or as a result of a problem? There is much to be gained and learned from solving problems.

HANDLING HIDDEN SOURCES OF TENSION

Sometimes it is easy to identify a problem, but sometimes factors of which we may not even be aware can become sources of tension. To improve our chances of keeping our home school on track, it may help to consider the following list. Perhaps unrecognized sources of difficulty can be corrected, perhaps preventive measures can be used. As in confronting any other problem, it helps to remember that there are always alternatives; if nothing else, a person can change his attitude and figure out a different way to view the situation.

--A child who has been home schooled may have a unique way of thinking. He may have a clarity of vision, a special confidence, a way of getting right to the heart of the matter, a disarming honesty, and incredible insight. He may be concerned with truth, not "the right answer;" he may not be afraid to own his thoughts, he may not be always looking over his shoulder asking, "Is this the right answer or should I guess again?" This unique approach may cause tension between a child and his parents who have not learned to think this way. Parents may get used to dealing with a person who thinks differently and accept the fact that sometimes their child can think more clearly than they can. They may learn some important things about thinking from their child.

--Parents who watch their child reaping the benefits of home schooling may at some point become angry because they were not home schooled themselves. They may regret the years they wasted in school and the effects it had on them. Recognizing this is often the first step toward resolving it, and some parents are grateful for the chance to experience the advantages of home schooling, even though they had to wait until they were adults to begin.

--Privacy can be a rare commodity for home schooling parents, and lack of privacy can cause frustration, especially in a society which says parents deserve lots of privacy from their children. Everyone needs some privacy, but some home schooling parents find it helps to insist on privacy only when they really need it. For example, if a parent begins dialing the phone, someone may ask, "Who are you calling?" and the parent may resent the fact that he cannot even make a phone call without being questioned. But if the parent instead tells anyone who looks interested, "I am going to call the garden center to see if they have cucumber seeds," the other person's curiosity is satisfied, and the parent has volunteered information rather than losing privacy. A child learns a lot from parents who are willing to share appropriate parts of their lives with her and often accepts her parents' need for privacy when she knows this is reserved for times when privacy is really essential, especially if her privacy is also respected.

--Some parents feel that food (especially sugar) can affect behavior. They make an effort to provide a well-balanced diet of whole natural foods and pleasant mealtimes, glad that home schooling gives them more influence over their child's diet.

CHAPTER 7

PARTICIPATING IN A SUPPORT GROUP

Support groups serve important functions. Many home schoolers value the opportunity to share ideas, experiences, and resources. It can be affirming and strengthening to talk with others about common values and concerns. Learning from other people's experiences can help new home schoolers get off to a good start. Children often benefit from a chance to meet and interact with other home schoolers; it helps them deal with "being different" from conventionally schooled children. Support groups also provide a means by which home schoolers can coordinate their efforts and work together to promote a favorable climate for home schooling and solve problems on the local and state level. Sometimes people who feel they are being forced into home schooling by threatened truancy prosecution or who are headed for legal difficulties for some reason are able to avoid problems because of what they learn from support group members and meetings.

A wide variety of activities can be carried out by support groups, if the members are interested. Some groups have primarily children's activities, such as field trips, arts and crafts, games, recreation, and guest speakers. Some emphasize meetings for parents. These may cover legal issues or alternative approaches to learning or provide opportunities to share experiences and concerns. Some groups publish a newsletter, and a phone tree makes communication rapid and effective. It helps a great deal to divide up the group work, so a number of people can participate and no one has too much to do.

To find a support group near you, contact your state home schooling organization or the publications listed in the Appendix. If there is not one in your area, consider organizing one yourself, even if you have never done anything like this before. Often it only takes one person to get things going.

CHAPTER 8

HIGH SCHOOL AND AFTER

CHOOSING A HIGH SCHOOL CURRICULUM

The variety of possible approaches to learning during the high school years may seem overwhelming, but it also provides important opportunities. Many teens begin by listing long-range goals, current interests, and activities (including work) they may want to pursue as an adult. Teens who do not have a specific goal may include exploring options as one objective. (In fact, given the number of people who change their minds and their careers, this might be a sensible goal for any teen.) Generally a teen realizes that some basic things are worth learning regardless of one's specific goal. Inability to read, write and do basic math imposes serious limitations, but even more important is learning how to learn. Many people include goals that are not strictly academic, such as learning to get along with a variety of people, run a household, repair a car.

Once goals have been listed (subject to modification as the need arises), it is easier to select an approach to learning. Many purchase and follow a prepared conventional curriculum. Possible advantages include: the planning and selection of materials are already done, required work is clearly defined and one knows when one is finished, the approach has been used by many people and is similar to that being used in conventional schools, it works well for some students, and some programs include the possibility of earning a diploma from a recognized high school. Possible disadvantages include the expense of the materials and the fact that this approach to learning does not work well for some and does not take full advantage of the flexibility and individualization that home schooling offers.

Another approach is to design a curriculum, suiting it to individual interests, strengths, abilities and goals, keeping in mind the legal requirements of your state. Subject matter and learning styles can be selected that allow a teen to pursue her interests and maximize her talents and abilities. The learning is relevant. Some students who have difficulty with conventional curriculums and approaches to learning become well motivated, successful learners. This approach, however, does require that a teen and her parent take more responsibility for planning, schedules, motivation, and problem solving and learn to live with some ambiguities, uncertainties, and the skepticism of others.

For some the best approach is a combination of these two approaches, such as studying math from a conventional text; taking a correspondence course in history; and learning reading and language arts by reading widely and writing letters, essays, and reports. Others choose to pursue a strong interest in depth, and find that this soon leads them into other basic subject areas as their competence and self-esteem increases.

Whatever the approach, it is important to include practical experience. Teens benefit from the opportunity to be of service and contribute, and they learn a great deal from interaction with others. Many also find employment rewarding for a number of reasons, assuming the job has been carefully selected. It costs money (for transportation, clothes, etc.) to make money, and the value of a teen's time needs to be weighed in determining whether a job is worthwhile.

THE QUESTION OF DIPLOMAS

Planning for a teen's diploma begins with the question of when or why a diploma will be required, since this will determine the type of diploma needed. Since some jobs, colleges, etc. do not require a diploma, some people do not need one.

Many conventional, recognized, and accredited schools award an official diploma to a home schooler who has met their graduation requirements. More flexible schools such as Clonlara (see Resources below) award diplomas on the completion of their less conventional requirements. Diplomas from these sources are widely recognized, but meeting the requirements costs time and money.

As far as we know, a home schooling family can set up its own graduation requirements and grant a diploma when they are met. Many conventional schools give one semester credit for 90 hours of class work plus homework, and some home schools use this as a guideline. Other ways of justifying a diploma include a specific list of books read, projects completed, etc.; examples of completed work; transcripts if correspondence or other formal courses have been taken; test scores if available; etc. These are possibilities, not requirements; remember that the purpose of a diploma is to convince someone that a person has the equivalent of a high school education, so think about what would be likely to convince your audience. Diploma forms can be purchased from a school supply house (see Resources) or individually prepared by a calligrapher. However, this type of diploma would be questioned and possibly rejected by some, especially since diplomas from small, "unaccredited" private schools are sometimes not acceptable.

A GED, obtained by taking a standardized test of General Educational Development (some states also have additional requirements), can sometimes be substituted for a high school diploma. For a person who already knows the material covered by the test (or who can master it using a preparatory book such as those listed in Resources below), this is a much quicker and less expensive way to obtain an "official" certificate than attending classes or taking correspondence courses. However, some individuals and institutions do not accept a GED (arguing that it is too easily obtained), and some home schoolers resist turning to the state as a judge and certifier of learning.

When high school is completed, some families celebrate with a graduation ceremony. This could be done for one student and could include such things as a rented cap and gown, guest speaker(s), musical performances by family members, special awards for younger children in the family, a reception for friends and relatives, and newspaper coverage.

SOCIALIZATION

"Sure, you can get a better education by studying at home, but what about your social life?" This is a question each teen and family must resolve; there are no easy answers. A few questions to ponder:

--Looking realistically at high schools in America today, would social life really be better if you were attending high school? What are you missing that is positive? That is negative? How would you handle the negative? What are the positive and negative aspects of home schooling that you would miss by going to school?

--What are alternative ways of meeting and interacting with other people? What is the value of spending time with people older and younger than you as well as with your peers?

--What other factors do you think you should consider? Where will you get the best education and have the best opportunity to do things that are really important to you?

See "Our Daughter's Perspective," pp. 78-80.

OPTIONS AFTER HIGH SCHOOL AT HOME

CONVENTIONAL COLLEGE

A few colleges welcome home schoolers, many are willing to accept them, and some home schoolers feel that any college so narrow-minded that it will not even consider home schoolers is probably not a place they would like anyway. It is generally a good idea to find out as early as possible what is required by colleges of the type you may want to attend.

In applying for admission, be up front and positive about home schooling; it can be presented as an advantage. Generally it works better to meet a college's requirements in your own way by fitting your experiences into the college's categories than to ignore requirements or ask that they be waived. For example, on a recommendation form to be filled out by a "high school counselor," a parent could write, "As John's father I have also functioned as his counselor. I find that he generally accepts responsibility well but...."

Standardized tests such as SAT and ACT are required by some colleges and can be a real asset for those who happen to be good at that kind of game. Otherwise one can find a college that does not require such tests or use the books listed under Resources for suggestions on preparing for such tests.

NON-TRADITIONAL COLLEGE

College credit and a recognized college degree can be earned from an accredited college on the basis of correspondence courses, tests such as CLEP and DANTE, and learning from life experience, which is documented in various ways. Although these programs were originally developed for adults, they are adaptable to home schoolers and are an excellent alternative for teens who prefer independent study and/or learning from experience. The

76

tremendous cost savings alone make them worth serious consideration, and John Bear's book is an excellent introduction.

EMPLOYMENT

Many alternatives exist, especially when home schooling is presented as an asset in a teen's background and effective ways are found to inform potential employers about learning which has been done. Richard Bolles' book presents ways of figuring out what kind of a job you would really like and finding and securing that job. The Whole Work Catalog lists books that stimulate thinking on jobs and work. Apprenticeships and internships may enable a teen to work and receive college credit at the same time.

MILITARY SERVICE

It appears (based on a few phone calls of inquiry) that a home schooler would be accepted into the military assuming he met other requirements. However, some recruiters seemed inclined to classify home schoolers as "high school drop-outs" unless they had a diploma based on graduation from high school and not on the GED. Since studies indicate that drop-outs are less likely to succeed in the military than high school graduates, such a classification could handicap a home schooler. Therefore someone seriously considering the military as an option should find out as soon as possible what the requirements are, including what kind of diploma would be acceptable.

OTHER ALTERNATIVES

Obviously we cannot cover everything that is available, such as volunteer service, missionary work, travel, homemaking, etc. These can be explored by using some variation of the pattern used to explore the options listed above: Gather information from as many sources as possible (books, people, etc.) to find out what options are already available. Consider alternatives with an open mind. If an option you would like is not currently available, figure out what it would take to make it available. When you meet an obstacle (notice that we did not say, "<u>If</u> you meet an obstacle..."), explore alternatives until you find a way around or through it, if possible. The fact that we are in relatively uncharted territory here means that sometimes things are more difficult, but there are also more opportunities. Sure it is hard work, but it is worth it! Home schooling during the high school years can be just as rewarding as earlier.

OUR DAUGHTER'S PERSPECTIVE

Since there is no perspective like that of someone who has been there, we asked our 18-year-old daughter to share some of her thoughts as she completed high school at home. She wrote about socialization:

When I was about eight and just starting home schooling, I thought that if I went back to public school (or any school, for that matter), I would have about ten really good friends (the kind that you tell everything to and who are always nice to you and you never get sick of). It was that simple. But I decided that maybe there were bad parts about school too, and that I did already have some friends, so I let the idea drop for a while.

Now at eighteen I have come to view meaningful friendships as something that requires a lot of time and effort. It is an ongoing process which going to school will not necessarily help at all.

"Socialization" in our society today has become equated with having a lot of peers with whom one has minimal contact (because of such limited time, etc.) but from whom one can claim friendship. In the area of tons of friends and lots of pressure from them, I have "missed being socialized," but healthy friendships (and sometimes it takes a long time to find/create one) require a lot more than simple acquaintance through school. The need for positive contact with other human beings is universal. Often people view it as something that one is either "given" or not. By going to school one is "given" the "socialization" necessary to be a "socialized person," people think, and yet we have a hard time figuring out what that means, and an even harder time becoming "socialized people."

As a home schooler I have always been asked about "socialization" or "making friends," more than any other question, and it has had many implications. "You're not going to be able to function in society because you have been kept away from it." "Well then you don't have any friends." "Because of you the society will be less able to get along." But most commonly, "Gee, it's too bad she doesn't have a chance to make lots of friends and have all the fun of school." At times I haven't minded the question; at other times I've hated it. But often I've wondered what will happen to this society if the way of being "socialized" is by attending school. Our society might be worried about anyone who isn't "socialized" because by not being "socialized" in the "regular way," the person could also be free from the trap that makes them conform within our society and thus not threaten its structure.

My idea of socialization includes being able to get along with people of all ages, races, cultures, etc. and in many different situations in which I am able to get away from being the peer or the daughter or the student or whatever and play other roles. Maybe I should call this "culturalization." In this area I feel that I have had a much more complete exposure to people, human interaction, and friendships than I ever would have had if I hadn't been home schooing. I've been able to work, learn, instruct, help, play, explore, etc., with all kinds of people at all ability levels, and these friendships I value very highly.

Home schooling has sometimes been thought of as something that keeps children separate from lots of peers and prevents peer pressure (it does, to some extent), but basically home schooling opens up a person's opportunities for interaction and helps people learn to interact in a society where we seem to have few good friendships, partly because people are labeled and categorized and put into boxes. This seems like a dangerous thing to have happen, and somehow as home schoolers we have to take on some responsibility for changing it. Human beings are meant to be integrated, not kept in boxes by age or other categories. But in order for integration to occur, children need to be given more respect and trust than they receive today.

As with any alternative, home schooling will always be looked upon as something that should be inspected, especially in the area of human relations. And being " socialized" is not as simple as knowing the alphabet, or being able to add. It is something that one has to continually relearn. A home schooler can expect that especially because she has been home schooled, she will be asked about it.

But really, I feel that my social interaction with people is what I value the most and the area in which I want to work the most. If people can get along and interact well together, then there must be hope for the world.

RESOURCES

This list of suggestions is a starting place; it is not exhaustive. A wide variety is included here to indicate the range of options available.

I. General information

A. *Growing Without Schooling*--A bimonthly magazine that includes articles by teens and their parents, many suggestions for activities and resources, and a mail order bookstore which carries some of the other resources listed here. 2269 Massachusetts Ave., Cambridge, MA 02140.

B. Nault, William H. "Typical Course of Study: Kindergarten through grade 12." Available for 50 cents from World Book, Inc., Merchandise Mart Plaza, Chicago, IL 60654. One example of a curriculum in outline form, but do conventional schools really cover everything that is listed here?

C. Pride, Mary. *The New Big Book of Home Learning* (covers the basics: reading, writing...) and *The Next Book of Home Learning* (covers "enrichment," such as foreign languages, business...). Good descriptions of learning materials, their costs and strengths and weaknesses, and how to get them.

II. Diplomas

A. Some home school curriculum packages include the option of receiving a diploma when the work has been completed.

B. Example of a school that will award a recognized diploma based on correspondences courses: University of Nebraska, High School Completion Program, Division of Continuing Studies, 511 Nebraska Hall, Lincoln, NE 68588.

C. Example of a school which will help develop an individualized high school curriculum and award an official diploma when it is completed: Clonlara School's Home-Based Education Program, 1289 Jewett, Ann Arbor, MI 48104.

D. Example of a supply house from which diplomas may be purchased: Supreme School Supply Co., 625 S. Dettloff Drive, P. O. Box 225, Arcadia, WI 54612.

E. Books to help prepare for the GED
1. *The Cambridge Pre-GED Program.* New York: Cambridge Book Co.
2. Scott, Foresman. *Passing the GED: A Complete Preparation Program for the High School Equivalency Examination.* Glenview, IL: Scott, Foresman and Co., 1987.

III. Attending a conventional college

A. General information
1. Gelner, Judy. *College Admissions: A Guide for Homeschoolers.* Sedalia, CO: Poppyseed Press, 1988. One family's experiences plus some general information. Somewhat helpful.

81

B. Preparing to take standardized tests

1. The College Board. *Ten SATs*. Actual SATs and suggestions for preparing to take the SAT.

2. Fiore, Neil and Susan C. Pescar. *Conquering Test Anxiety: or How To Psyche Up for the SAT, GRE, GMAT, LSAT, MCAT, or Any Other Standardized Test*. NY: Warner Books, 1987.

3. Robinson, Adam and John Katzman. *Cracking the System: The SAT*. NY: Villard Books, 1986. Excellent guide to preparing for the SAT.

IV. Non-traditional college

A. Books

1. Bear, John. *How to Get the Degree You Want: Bear's Guide to Non-Traditional College Degrees*. Berkeley, CA: Ten Speed Press. Excellent starting place and general guide to non-traditional degrees. Bibliography, many addresses, etc.

2. Hawes, Gene R. *Getting College Course Credits by Examination to Save $$$*. NY: McGraw-Hill, 1979. Descriptions (including some sample questions) of tests and suggestions for preparing for them.

3. *Peterson's Independent Study Catalog*. Listing of hundreds of academic courses on the high school, college, and graduate level.

4. Rushing, Brian C., ed. *1990 Internships: 38,000 On-the-Job Training Opportunities for Students and Adults*. Cincinnati: Writer's Digest Books, 1989. Brief descriptions of organizations that offer internships, requirements, how to apply, etc.

5. Simosko, Susan. *Earn College Credit For What You Know*. Washington, DC: Acropolis Books Ltd., 1985. Excellent guide to getting credit for learning through life experience. Covers identifying what was learned, documenting it, etc. Examples and worksheets included.

B. Addresses of testing companies

1. College-Level Examination Program (CLEP), DANTES, and Advanced Placement Program (APP) are all handled by Educational Testing Service, Princeton, NJ 08541.

2. ACT-Proficiency Examination Program (ACT-PEP), American College Testing Program, P.O. Box 168, Iowa City, IA 52243.

V. Employment

A. Bolles, Richard. *The 1989 What Color Is Your Parachute? A Practical Manual for Job-Hunters and Career Changers.* Berkeley, CA: Ten Speed Press, 1989.

B. *The Whole Work Catalog,* Box 297-UE, Boulder, CO 80306. Books about a wide variety of work options; many alternatives.

C. Also see Rushing's *Internships* under Part IV Non-traditional college above.

PART III

THE ROLE OF HOME SCHOOLING IN AMERICAN EDUCATION

CHAPTER 9

POLITICAL REALITY AND POLITICAL ACTION

The American educational system is not an independent force in our society; it does not operate on the basis of decisions that will maximize the learning opportunities that are available to children. Instead it is dominated by government bureaucracy, by special interest groups, and by the needs and values of big business. Because education is so bound by the political system, home schoolers need to become politically active in order to be able to reclaim and maintain their right to home school without harmful government regulation that will force home schools to become like conventional schools.

DOMINANCE OF EDUCATION BY GOVERNMENT, BUSINESS, AND EDUCATIONAL INTEREST GROUPS

Basically home schooling in America today is a political issue because education in general has become extremely political. There is nothing inevitably political about either education in general or home schooling in particular. In fact, in some societies education goes on independent of the political system; children are either educated at home by their parents or in private schools. (To be sure, not many societies operate this way today, but it is important to realize that this has worked very well and, according to some, is a highly desirable situation.)

American education became inextricably bound up with the political system during the nineteenth century when the ideas of free public education and compulsory school attendance were widely promoted. Although some people supported these ideas because they honestly believed they would be helpful to children, the real impetus came from the newly industrialized economic system that needed trained workers. To have compulsory school attendance laws, the government had to provide free public education for all children. It was decided that this was best done by financing schools with tax money, and when the government began funding schools, it gained a very strong measure of control over them. Business interests strongly influenced the shaping of these schools. The idea was that children would be compelled to attend factory modeled schools to prepare for largely routinized jobs.

To counter the influence of business in education, teachers have organized unions because they can have greater influence on the government's educational policy as a group than they could as individuals. (Other groups involved in education, such as administrators and school board members, have also formed associations to advance their self-interests. These are a factor in American education today [see pp. 133-136], but their numbers are smaller and their influence is not as great as that of the teachers unions.) Teachers as a group have a great deal of political power because of their numbers, because they are more or less evenly distributed throughout legislative districts, and because they are generally educated and articulate individuals. Teachers unions have turned this potential into a powerful political force. The unions have a great deal of money from membership dues, and this plus the voting power of teachers enables unions to strongly influence legislative elections. Therefore they have a good chance to elect legislators who will then vote the way the unions want them to. Teachers unions are also often able to control appointments to the education committees of state legislatures and thus block legislation they do not like.

One serious problem with this whole system is that teachers unions naturally have represented only the interests of teachers (at least their salary, benefits, and tenure interests). No such organized groups argue for the interests of students, or families, or society as a whole, and the interests of these other groups often conflict with those of teachers.

It is important to distinguish between the beliefs and actions of teachers unions and of individual teachers. Many teachers are much more reasonable, fair, and balanced in their approach to educational policy than is the leadership of the unions. Such teachers make strong allies of home schoolers and need support and information from home schoolers.

Despite the success of the teachers unions, business interests still exercise a strong influence over education. Actually, this is not surprising. Although businesses and teachers unions are often at odds over distribution and use of money for education, both subscribe to values and tactics that put their own self-interest ahead of the needs of children and are not supportive of either families in general or home schoolers in particular.

Education in contemporary America has also become heavily involved in the economic system. One fifth of the labor force is directly or indirectly involved in education, and one billion dollars are spent on education every day. This is not inevitable; when children are simply educated at home in the course of their daily lives, education can maintain its independence of big business and educational interest groups. But in America, education has become a big business. Decisions regarding education have major economic implications. People cannot decide to do something different, like home school, without causing concern among people who make their money from the current educational system.

WHY HOME SCHOOLERS NEED TO BE POLITICALLY ACTIVE

Because education in America today is so dominated by the political system, the decision to home school is a political decision.

Therefore, home schoolers need to be aware of the political dimensions of their actions, rather than just making decisions without thinking about the political consequences. If we do not become aware and politically active, we will be swallowed by the educational system and the forces that are driving it.

Becoming actively involved in the political process is not easy for many home schoolers. We are too busy, or not interested, or lack the experience and self-confidence to step into the political arena. Politics today has a bad reputation, too, as many people feel powerless to affect the system in any significant way. But we have no choice--if we home schoolers do not work to preserve and defend our rights, to prevent unreasonable home schooling laws from being passed, no one else will defend us and we will lose badly.

However reluctant we may be initially, we home schoolers can be effective once we become politically active for several reasons. We are a strongly committed group fighting for something we care about deeply. Home schoolers have consistently done a good job of educating children, as shown by the successes of former home schoolers who have entered conventional schools, favorable reports about home schoolers in the press, and personal observations of home schoolers by relatives, friends, and neighbors. Public sympathy is often on the side of home schoolers, especially when we show what a good job we are doing and how unreasonably we are being treated by the educational bureaucracy. Many people recognize the justice of our cause. In addition, although teachers unions are formidable opponents, they are not invincible. Many teachers are not politically active, and others disagree with the positions of the union leadership and do not follow orders. It is unusual for a legislator to get more than five to eight letters from individuals on an issue, so it does not take large numbers to make an impression, provided these are thoughtful, well-informed letters and not simply signatures at the bottom of a form letter.

There are four major reasons why home schoolers need to become politically active. First, because of opposition to home

90

schooling, our freedom to home school without unreasonable restriction will be lost unless we actively counter this opposition. Second, there are trends in American education today which do not directly involve home schoolers but which have the potential to cause home schoolers great harm. Political means can be used to counter these trends. Third, there are trends in American education which home schoolers could support, draw on, and use. Fourth, home schoolers have the potential to make an important contribution to American education today, but they must become politically active to accomplish this.

The first step in responsible political action is to understand these factors. Below is a discussion of each.

THE NEED TO COUNTER OPPOSITION TO HOME SCHOOLING

Before we can effectively counter the opposition to home schooling, we need to understand it and its basis for opposing home schooling. For clarity, this opposition is divided into two groups, that which is an unintentional by-product of other trends or factors in education and that which is specifically and deliberately directed against home schooling.

UNINTENTIONAL OPPOSITION

The opposition to home schooling that appears to be unintentional, simply a product of "the way things are" in our society today, can be seen in the following examples.

--A society driven by money and power is very suspicious of approaches that differ from the norm and might lead to independent thinking. The need for social control severely limits the amount of freedom that can be allowed for alternatives. In addition, the educational establishment has so much political power and involves so much money that members of the establishment have become very jealous and protective of their territory. There are no real effective checks and balances to the power, control, and authority of the educational establishment.

--Inertia is on the side of conventional schooling, since it is the status quo, and opposed to home schooling, which represents change. Commonly held assumptions about education work against home schooling. Among the highly misleading assumptions that are commonly made: First, children will not learn unless they are taught and tested by specially trained personnel. Second, parents cannot educate their own children because they love them and are not "objective" about them. Third, children should be doing school work between 9 AM and 3 PM. Fourth, school is essential for a child to become socialized. Fifth, conventional outcomes of education (diplomas, credentials, licensing, etc.) are needed for America to compete internationally. These assumptions are clearly false and have been disproved many times, but they are still widespread and work against home schoolers.

--There is a certain prejudice against home schoolers because they are "different," "weird," etc.

INTENTIONAL OPPOSITION

Other opposition is clearly and deliberately directed against home schoolers. For example,

--The educational establishment objects to anything or anyone that might threaten its power and control. It strongly resists allowing anything "educational" to exist outside its power and control.

--Professional interest groups such as teachers unions fear the loss of jobs, income, and prestige if home schooling spreads too much.

--Some school officials have a mistaken notion that they are responsible for seeing that all children, including home schoolers, get educated. In fact, they appear to worry more about home schoolers than students in conventional schools.

COUNTERING OPPOSITION

Both the unintentional and the deliberate opposition can be countered in two basic ways. First, home schoolers can try to win the hearts and minds of the general public by convincing people that home schooling is a workable alternative and should be accepted as such and not overly regulated. Second, home schoolers can engage in on-going legislative battles to keep the opposing forces at bay and protect their rights. The first approach is the real solution, but the second is necessary as a stop-gap measure until the first is accomplished. Or, should the first prove to be impossible, the second would be the best means of defense. The first approach is covered in Part IV of this book, the second in Part V.

TRENDS IN AMERICAN EDUCATION

Home schooling does not exist in a vacuum. It is seen as part of the American educational system and so is affected by it. Things that are required or expected of conventional school students become expectations of home schoolers. For example, the increase in standardized testing requirements for public school students has resulted in increased pressure for state-mandated standardized testing of home schoolers. Therefore, it is important that home schoolers be aware of changes in the conventional educational system and, when possible, influence them.

However, it is not easy to gain a clear picture of what is really happening in American education today. Leaders of the educational establishment present changes they favor in ways that will make them most acceptable to the general public. Some changes might generate strong opposition were they presented clearly; these are quietly arranged. And of course different people have different perspectives on what the goals of the educational system should be. The next two sections then present what will no doubt be a somewhat controversial analysis of what is happening in American education today and what should be done about it.

CURRENT TRENDS THAT COULD BE HARMFUL TO HOME SCHOOLERS

Two major trends in American education today could harm home schoolers directly or indirectly. First, the state is increasingly assuming responsibility for raising children, taking this responsibility away from parents. There is a growing movement to transfer family rights and responsibilities away from the family and into larger institutions under professional control or at least to ensure that professionals are passing judgment on the family's competency and behavior. This is being accomplished in a variety of ways, including:

--Early childhood education is growing, including full-day kindergarten for 5 year olds and publicly funded kindergarten for 4 year olds. Even more problematic, the idea that children benefit from formal schooling at age 3 or 4 is spreading.

--Day care facilities located in public schools, even if they are privately run and independent of the schools, represent the schools' taking over or becoming the focus of the family function of caring for and nurturing the very young.

--The number of years covered by the compulsory school attendance law has been increased in some states by requiring that children either begin school at an earlier age or stay in school longer (till age 18 or so) or both.

--A growing distrust of the ability of parents to raise their children can be seen in state-run family resource centers and parental training programs. These are voluntary at present but some may become mandatory in the future. There is something frightening about state-run programs to teach parents about parenting, even if they are voluntary. There has also been a tremendous increase in guidance counselors, social workers, and special education professionals.

The second major trend in American education today that could harm home schoolers directly or indirectly is the increasing standardization of public education. This is a serious concern for home schoolers. As public education becomes more standardized, the idea will grow that everyone should have the same education. This will put more pressure on home schools to prove that they are equivalent to these standardized public schools and that they offer the same educational "opportunity" in the areas of treatment of special problems or what so-called "professional experts" have defined as social, mental, emotional, or physical needs.

Among the factors that are contributing to the increasing standardization of American education are:

--Requirements that public schools use a standardized curriculum. (For example, in 1983 the U. S. Department of Education published *A Nation at Risk,* which described how poorly schools were doing, using standardized test scores as the primary evidence. As a result, between 1983 and 1989, 35 states enacted legislation and/or regulations requiring that public schools further standardize their curriculums.)

--Requirements that public schools administer standardized tests. In 1972 only one state mandated standardized testing; by 1985, 35 states did; and by 1989, all 50 states did. Since teachers try to prepare students for the tests they will have to take, the use of standardized tests dictates and standardizes curriculum.

--Establishment of detailed procedures to manage large school systems and emulate modern industrial practices by achieving economies of scale. In an educational system, this means trying to reduce the cost of educating each student by treating all the students in the same way, as if they were identical pieces on an assembly line.

--Loss of local control of education as state bureaucracies dictate policies to local school boards and local school officials.

--An increasing reliance on quantitative measures of "education," such as number of hours spent in school, scores on standardized tests, and credits earned, in an attempt to hold schools accountable.

--Increased labeling of students who deviate from the standard as "learning disabled," "at risk," etc., segregating them from other students, and treating them in programs run by "educational specialists." (Over 10% of all students are now in special education.)

There are several ways home schoolers can respond to the state's taking increasing responsibility for children and to the increasing standardization of public education.

(1) We can ignore the situation and hope it will not affect us very seriously very soon.

(2) We can make sure that we ourselves are accurately informed about these trends and make others aware of them.

(3) We can make sure that the candidates and programs we support will move the educational system in the direction that we feel it needs to go and will not foster the trends we oppose. We can communicate to our legislators our feelings and beliefs on these issues and urge them to vote in ways that will support our positions.

(4) We can maintain a clear sense that we are not part of the public educational system and not allow ourselves to be carried along with these harmful developments. We can take seriously

the opportunity that we have to be an alternative to the system and preserve and protect at least a small area in which children are treated as unique and valuable individuals within strong and thriving families.

TRENDS WHICH HOME SCHOOLERS COULD SUPPORT AND USE

The American educational system is large and complex. Although there are serious negative trends, positive things are also happening. Some of these deserve and will benefit from the support of home schoolers; other can be pointed to and used by home schoolers to support attempts to maintain a climate of opinion favorable to home schooling. Among the examples and ways in which positive trends can be used by home schoolers:

--Several states, including New Jersey, Texas, California, and Florida have recently reduced or considered reducing certification requirements for public school teachers. For example, a Texas law prohibits the state from requiring more than 18 credit hours in teacher training for certification. Major commission reports such as the Carnegie Forum on Education and the Economy's *A Nation Prepared: Teachers for the 21st Century* have recommended abolishing undergraduate degree programs in teacher education. Home schoolers who are threatened with the possibility that their state might require the certification of home schooling parents can argue that they should not be saddled with requirements which are being questioned and reduced.

--Many people are pointing out the dangers of standardized tests and the damage they do and instead are supporting the use of alternatives such as portfolio evaluations and outcome or performance assessments. Home schoolers fighting state-mandated standardized testing can cite these examples. (For details see pp. 166-168.)

--A few states are moving away from standardized textbooks and curriculums and are allowing more local control and variation. For example, California allows 20% of its curriculum budget to be spent on trade books rather than required standardized texts. Also, Washington state allows school districts to request exemptions from state mandates so they can try new approaches. Home schoolers can point to this evidence of the need for alternatives in education.

--New alternatives and options are being allowed within the public education system in some places. For example, a state program in Minnesota provides high school juniors and seniors the option of taking one or all of their courses in a public or private college or university with monies from the public school covering costs of tuition, books, and transportation. Wisconsin's pilot school choice program for Milwaukee gives parents of low income public school students the opportunity to send their child to a non-sectarian private school by providing the school with up to $2,500 of public school monies for each child. (The program is limited to 1,000 students.) In East Harlem, New York City, a high school's curriculum, course offerings, school day, and teaching were radically altered by a program which included team teaching, peer teaching, and independent study. Before beginning the program, less than 10% of the seniors graduated from high school; as a result of the program over 90% went to college. One of the biggest challenges and costs was re-educating teachers so they developed new attitudes and approaches to teaching.

--Some conventional schools are encouraging children to explore a variety of learning styles and offering children opportunities to learn in ways besides paper, pencil, and books. Thomas Armstrong's *In Their Own Way* stresses the importance of conventional schools' encouraging a variety of approaches to learning.

--New evidence is being published which supports the old and widely recognized fact that parents are the primary educators of their children, even if the children attend conventional schools. For example, Anne T. Henderson's *Evidence Continues to Grow:*

Parent Involvement Improves Student Achievement reviews and summarizes 53 studies and shows that parents are the key to student learning. Writing in the *Journal of Economic Literature* (September, 1986), Eric A. Hanushek critiques 147 studies that sought to correlate student achievement with a wide variety of school-related factors including teacher certification and advanced degrees, curriculum, time on task, quality of the facility, expenditures, class size, etc. The single variable that consistently correlated positively with student achievement was family background. (We recognize that most if not all of such studies are highly questionable, especially since they rely on standardized tests to measure achievement and also equate achievement with learning. Our point here is that much of what passes for the soundest educational research indicates that the family rather than the school correlates with academic achievement.)

--Many people are recognizing the problems with the diagnosis and treatment of "learning disabled" children and others in special education. Gerald S. Coles' *Learning Mystique*, a comprehensive study of the literature on learning disabilities, concludes that there is no reliable method or technique for identifying learning disabilities. LaVaun Dennett, Principal at Montlake Elementary School, an inner city school in Seattle, tried the "radical" experiment of removing learning disability labels and mainstreaming special education teachers and students. The experiment, a remarkable success, has been expanded to 21 other schools.

--States, institutions, and many individuals are recognizing the problems with early academic pressure on pre-school and kindergarten children. A task force on early childhood education in California has recommended less academic pressure in the early years. The American Academy of Pediatrics was reported to be issuing a warning paper on the health risks associated with early childhood education. North Carolina has banned standardized testing through the second grade, and similar legislation has been introduced in several other states. David Elkind, President of the National Association for the Education of Young Children, has stated that there is no evidence that early childhood education has long-term benefits.

Home schoolers can respond to these positive trends in a number of ways.

--The more we can document the disagreements that exist among conventional school "experts," the more strongly we can argue that we need to be left alone because they do not have "the truth."

--We can support these trends in whatever way possible, including informing other people about them, speaking in support of them, encouraging legislators to introduce and support such measures, etc.

--We can point out that home schoolers have been arguing for and practicing many of these things for many years. Obviously we strongly support parental involvement in education, we encourage alternative learning styles and approaches to education, etc. People concerned about education should realize that home schoolers are on the forefront of innovative educational developments; they should try to learn from us instead of trying to regulate us.

--We can look to these positive examples so we do not repeat mistakes conventional schools have made in the past. We can also argue that practices that conventional schools are now questioning (standardized testing, certification of teachers, etc.) should not be required of home schoolers.

CONTRIBUTIONS HOME SCHOOLERS COULD MAKE TO AMERICAN SOCIETY

Home schoolers have the potential to make important contributions to American education today, but we must become politically active to accomplish this. There are numerous possibilities, including:

--Home schoolers know a great deal about children's learning. We do not have to deal with many of the distracting problems that conventional school personnel encounter, such as: discipline problems; the need for fixed schedules; the need to keep the administration, the school board, and the taxpayers happy; pressure from teachers unions; requirements from the state educational bureaucracy; etc. Therefore we are able to focus on children's learning, and we could share a great deal with conventional educators about ways of facilitating children's learning; of encouraging them to explore alternative ways of learning; of helping them discover where their real strengths, talents, and abilities lie; etc. To be sure, some of the approaches that work so well in a home school would not be directly transferrable to a conventional school because the basic structure of the school is so different, but home schoolers still have a lot to share with conventional school personnel.

--Another important lesson conventional schools could learn from home schools is how important parental involvement is in a child's education and how well it works. When so many home schooling parents are taking full responsibility for their children's educations and handling it so well, conventional schools could certainly involve parents much more freely and deeply in the education of their children.

--Home schoolers' experiences and knowledge about learning could also be used to help policy makers trust parents.

--Home schoolers' experiences could be used to demonstrate that dollars should be transferred away from educational and social welfare institutions and back to the family. Reliance on factory modeled, highly bureaucratic and specialized institutions is costing huge amounts of money and destroying many children's desire or ability to learn, despite the fact that the family has consistently been shown to be more effective in caring for and educating children. (Any transfer of money, however, would need to be on the basis that families were free to care for and educate their children as they saw fit. Allowing professional day care or educational interests to regulate what families did with the money or to certify them before they received money would impose the very practices that have proven destructive to the family and to education.)

--Home schoolers stand on the forefront of freedom in education today. We are one of the groups that is most strongly resisting the increasing standardization of education and the increasing attempts of the educational establishment to take over the functions of the family. If home schoolers can resist the opposition that would use regulation by the state to force us to become like conventional schools, we can make an important contribution to maintaining some freedom in the educational system and to strengthening the family, which is vital to our survival as a society. But if home schoolers are destroyed through regulation that turns home schools into carbon copies of conventional schools, then government, business, and teachers unions will have even more control over the educational system and will be in a position to extend their dominance by moving next against small private schools, and then on further. Our battle as home schoolers is not just for our own rights; it is for the preservation of a free society. We need and deserve the support of non-home schoolers who are concerned about education and our future as a nation.

CONCLUSION

Because American education today is so dominated by the political system, we home schoolers need to be politically active in order to protect our rights and survive as an alternative in education. Understanding how the system operates and what opposition we face is the first step; a brief outline has been presented here which home schoolers can expand as we do further reading and act politically. Suggestions for effective ways of becoming politically active are presented in succeeding parts of this book.

CHAPTER 10

CHALLENGES FACING HOME SCHOOLERS

When we look at the whole picture of the political situation in which home schoolers find themselves today, there are major challenges which will test us in the coming months and years. Several are discussed here.

FORCING HOME SCHOOLS TO BECOME LIKE CONVENTIONAL SCHOOLS

Home schools are seriously threatened by efforts of the educational establishment to make home schools like conventional schools through regulation. When the number of home schoolers clearly began to increase again during the 1970's (remember home schooling is the traditional approach to education that has been used throughout most of human history), there were debates about whether home schooling was legal or should be allowed at all. These have now clearly been settled in favor of home schoolers; no legislative attempts are being made to outlaw home schooling. However, the educational establishment seems to have decided, consciously or unconsciously, that having lost that battle, they will now proceed to win the war by regulating home schools until they become like conventional schools.

Some home schoolers feel that if we just accepted one major regulation and showed the educational establishment and the general public once and for all that we are legitimate, that our children score well on standardized tests (or whatever other standard was chosen), then the battle would be over, we would have shown other people (and ourselves) that we are doing a good job, and we could quietly continue to home school. But this is not what would happen. As soon as we made one concession, another would be demanded of us. This process would continue until the educational establishment had firm control over home schools. Also home schoolers know that one of the real strengths of home schools is their flexibility and ability to meet the unique needs of individual children. Increased regulation would ruin home schools.

Are home schoolers willing to become like conventional schools or are we going to fight efforts to further regulate home schools?

GRASSROOTS ORGANIZATIONS

If home schoolers want to fight unreasonable regulations, we must work through grassroots organizations. We do not have the numbers or the money or the political power to challenge the educational establishment head-on. Also, home schooling regulations are found in state laws and in local school board policies, so we need to work on the local and state level.

We must do this work ourselves, each of us active, involved, and doing our part. We cannot rely on "outside experts" who come into a state to help. We must not allow someone else (whether from within the state or from outside) to take care of our interests for us by claiming to represent all home schoolers and then serving on a legislative committee or working behind closed doors to develop a home schooling law or to act in other ways that supposedly protect our interests. If we do this, we risk surrendering our independence, our self-esteem, and our political

105

power to the person who claimed to be there to help us. We lose control of our lives, we lose the sense that we are responsible for ourselves, and we lose confidence that we can fight our own battles. It would be better, personally and politically, to work as a grassroots movement to fight our own battle and if necessary succumb to a terrible law which our consciences would require that we not obey. Even this would be better than having our freedoms compromised by allowing someone else to do our work for us and by this act be given legitimacy in the eyes of our adversaries, the general public, and most unfortunately, ourselves. For it is not merely political folly to think that one person could be strong enough or wise enough to do what really can only be done by many people working together to protect their freedom; it would mean that our effort at political empowerment had turned into dependency and humiliation.

Are home schoolers willing to establish and work through grassroots organizations?

THE PROBLEM WITH VOUCHERS FOR HOME SCHOOLS

Home schoolers may be offered a chance to participate in a voucher system. At first glance, a voucher system appears to have many advantages: the government would give each family the money it would have spent on a public school education for the family's children, and the family could use this money to educate their children in any way they chose. It sounds like a home schooler's dream--to actually get paid for home schooling. However, in reality it is clear that vouchers would not be allowed to be used for home schooling unless the government had strong control over home schools, unless there were strong regulations being strictly enforced, unless home schoolers could prove that their children were really getting a good education. Therefore home schoolers are forced to conclude that the only way they could participate in a voucher system would be to pay for it with their freedom.

Are home schoolers willing to submit to further regulation in order to participate in a voucher program?

NEED FOR AN INDEPENDENT DEFINITION OF HOME SCHOOLING

As home schooling gains recognition and acceptance, the definition of what home schooling is and what home schoolers do is becoming narrower and more limited. Before many people had heard of home schooling, the few who chose this educational alternative could select whatever approach to education they wanted, because no one had a clear expectation of what home schooling really was anyway. But now that home schooling is receiving much more publicity, there is a very real danger that a rigid definition of home schooling will develop. If it does, home schoolers will lose important freedoms, because in essence society will say, "It is all right if you home school as long as you do it according to our expectations, as long as your home school is very much like a conventional school, with a standardized curriculum and children who score well on standardized tests." Home schooler who do not want home schooling to be limited in this way need to work to help forge a definition of home schooling that is not based on conventional school standards.

Among the points worth considering regarding a definition of home schooling are the following:

--The definition should be broad enough to include the very wide range of approaches to home schooling that exists. There should be room for home schoolers who want to come as close as possible to duplicating what conventional schools do as well as for home schoolers who want to encourage their children to learn in unconventional ways, pursuing their own interests and learning at their own pace. The definition should also encompass the wide range of religious beliefs and lifestyles that are found among home schoolers.

--The definition of home schooling should not be based on what conventional schools do. By their nature and character, home schools are very different from conventional schools. Having few students of varying ages with close ties to the "teacher" makes a tremendous difference in how and when learning occurs and what restrictions must be placed on children. Of course some home schoolers may want to borrow ideas about curriculum, teaching methods, etc. from conventional schools, but duplication of conventional school approaches to education should not be a primary means of defining a home school.

--The definition should acknowledge that each family has the right to make its own decisions concerning the education of its children. Each family is also in the best position to make decisions concerning approaches to learning, subject matter to be studied, pace at which children should learn, etc. Home schoolers should not let themselves be put in the position of judging other home schoolers.

--To forge a new definition, home schoolers should be willing to depart from the seemingly safe confines of conventional schooling; to try new ideas; to take risks; to work without support from others; and to endure questioning, criticism, and sometimes outright ridicule.

--This new definition must emerge from the grassroots level of home schooling. It cannot be formulated by any expert or home schooling organization or book. It has to grow gradually as many parents learn with their children, ponder what they see happening, and share their ideas and experiences with other home schoolers.

Are home schoolers willing to unite to meet this challenge?

PART IV

WINNING SUPPORT FOR HOME SCHOOLING

CHAPTER 11

POLITICAL EMPOWERMENT OF HOME SCHOOLERS

This chapter shows how rights are lost, how people can protect their rights, why it is so important that home schoolers remain united, and how unity can be maintained. Attention is also given to two strategies that can cause serious problems for home schoolers: relying on outside experts and relying too heavily on legal (including constitutional) arguments. Subsequent chapters contain more practical information on how to gather information, choose a strategy for changing educational policy, and develop and maintain a grassroots organization.

HOW RIGHTS ARE LOST

To understand why it is so important that home schoolers (and others) work to protect their rights and responsibilities in education, it may help to look at some of the ways in which these can easily be lost.

--Rights can be lost when people become conditioned to believing pronouncements made by authorities, experts, and professionals rather than trusting their own observations, judgments, and common sense. People may even begin to accept misleading or inaccurate statements, against their better judgment, partly because they have lost self-confidence or feel powerless to do otherwise. For example, people may not question a public school official's statement that the state is responsible for a child's education.

--Rights can also be lost when people do not know what their rights are and do not exercise them but instead accept conventional opinion and behavior concerning parental rights and the importance of parental involvement in a child's education. Sometimes people simply do what everyone else is doing, without question. For example, they may allow their five year old to be screened for mental, psychological, social, and physical development rather than refusing to participate in a voluntary and potentially harmful test. (See pp. 258-262 for more about preschool screening.)

--Rights can be lost when people abdicate their responsibilities and look for someone else to take care of a situation. This is particularly tempting when there are problems or when a person begins to question something she has been doing. For example, when there is a threat of legislation that would regulate home schoolers, a home schooler may decide to wait and see what happens rather than working to educate the community and media about the issue and meeting with her legislator.

It is important that home schoolers be aware of the need to act to maintain rights and responsibilities, because we face outright opposition to home schooling and because we are bound up in the educational system and risk losing our rights and freedom as the other members of this system lose theirs in trends that include the state's taking over family rights and responsibilities and a movement toward increasing standardization. (Opposition to home schooling and trends in education are discussed in Chapter 9 above.)

WAYS OF PROTECTING RIGHTS AND RESPONSIBILITIES

There are two major things which we can do to protect our rights and responsibilities. First, we need to learn as much as we can about our own situation, about opposition we must guard against and overcome, about options and alternatives that are available, and about strategies that may work. Ways of gathering information are discussed in Chapter 12, and options for changing educational policy are covered in Chapter 13. Second, people need to join with others who have similar concerns, commitments, and goals. They need to network, support each other, and work together in grassroots organizations. Information about existing organizations may be obtained from the national publications listed in Appendix A. Chapter 14 has suggestions for developing and maintaining grassroots home schooling organizations.

As people join together, results such as these occur: Home schoolers and others become better educated about the law and important issues. School officials realize that home schoolers know the law and will take action. A record and/or precedent is set that can be used in the future. Actions contrary to the intent of the law are less likely to continue and become further ingrained in people's minds and actions. Individual rights are less likely to be taken away. Others will learn from and follow this example.

IMPORTANCE OF UNITY AMONG HOME SCHOOLERS

Unity among home schoolers is essential for us to maximize our strength. We must unite to affirm parents' responsibility for their children's education and to protect the right of parents to educate their children at home if they so choose. We must avoid taking a stand on potentially divisive issues such as what approach to learning is best; what specific techniques should be used in home schooling; whether a purchased curriculum should be used and if so, which one.

113

Home schoolers have many different loyalties and commitments. Our own families are extremely important to us; that is one of the main reasons we are home schooling. We feel strongly about our right to choose for our children the best possible education for them, consistent with our beliefs and principles. We have strong ideas and convictions about the particular approach to education that we have chosen for our own family.

Sometimes our loyalties and commitments seem to conflict with each other, and we have to figure out a way to order them so they do not interfere with each other. Many home schoolers believe that political questions in general are not the most important questions in life and do not think that the legal right to home school without undue state regulation is the most important issue people will ever face or the most important problem they will ever confront. But in order to be able to deal with questions that really matter, questions of approaches to education and even larger questions of religious faith, belief, and moral values and principles, we have to have the political freedom and right to home school without undue interference from the state. Therefore we must all work together to regain and maintain our legal right to home school, regardless of the reasons any of us as individuals has for exercising this right and regardless of the approach we choose for educating our children. We must not insist that every home schooler agree on just one approach to education, religion, or moral values, and we must fight for the right of home schoolers and others to make these decisions for themselves.

This seems backwards. But by putting a less important question first in time (by working as a united group of home schoolers to assure our right to home school before dividing up into smaller groups in which the members agree about approaches to education, religion, moral values), we are really giving the most important questions the value and priority they so justly deserve. If we took the other approach, if we first split into smaller groups of people who agreed about educational and religious matters, we would not be able to withstand the political pressures from those who oppose home schooling. We would soon be living under

114

repressive home schooling laws which would place unnecessarily restrictive regulations on home schoolers. (Look at the home schooling laws in states in which home schoolers have become divided or were never united.) We all need time and energy to decide about educational and religious questions and act on them. But we would have to spend much of that time and energy fighting the results of repressive legislation, meeting ridiculous requirements that we "prove" to school officials that we are truly educating our children (this would, of course, have to be according to their standards--too bad for us if we happen to disagree with them!) and/or staying out of court and possibly even jail.

In addition to the practical need to remain united, there is a more fundamental reason why we should not try to get all home schoolers to agree on curriculums, approaches to education, learning techniques, etc. There is no one answer that is right for everyone. Each family must decide for itself what is most important and works best when it comes to the specifics of home schooling. A common objection to conventional schools is that they do not allow enough flexibility to meet the widely varying needs of different individuals. This is also why many people are concerned about the increasing standardization and centralization of the public schools. So let us welcome diversity, respect our differences, learn from each other, and remain united.

Home schoolers from very different backgrounds and with different beliefs and aspirations need to say that our freedom to home school our children is more important than our differences. In a sense, we are also saying, "My principles and beliefs are strong enough to withstand your principles and beliefs being felt and expressed more fully." Or, in other words, the fundamental freedom we share must be protected so we can each act on our individual beliefs, for without this freedom we would all be less than we can be with it.

THE RISKS OF RELYING ON OUTSIDE EXPERTS

It is important to realize that we home schoolers do not need experts. We rely on our own knowledge and abilities, which are considerable. We do our own careful ground work, we watch carefully and constantly for new developments, we fight our own battles, and we live with the results.

Of course this kind of "stubborn independence" can be carried too far. There is much to be learned from the ideas and experiences of other home schoolers and home schooling organizations around the country. This kind of communication is positive and benefits us all. But we need to be careful not to become dependent on "outside experts," people working on the national level who would come in and "solve" our problems for us. There are a number of reasons why such reliance is unwise and does not work well.

--Using outside experts decreases the commitment and energy that members of a grassroots organization put into the work that must be done, thus weakening the organization.

--Much of the success of home schoolers and our organizations depends on the reputation we have established. It is important to be seen as responsible and committed people who know what we are talking about. It is also important to develop contacts throughout a state with whom we can work on a personal basis. An outside expert simply does not have the time or ability to do this kind of careful groundwork.

--People who live in a state inevitably know and understand it better than an outside expert. We can work with legislators in our own state who strongly disagree with us because underneath our differences, we all live in the same state and we all care about its future. (Of course our commitment to the state we live in is not our highest commitment, but it is a significant one.) Obviously an outside expert cannot have this kind of a bond with legislators, simply because she does not live in the state.

--Legislators view outside experts differently than they view us, their constituents. Once an "expert" is called in, a legislator's role shifts from champion of minority-interest constituents to judge of claims made by experts in response to competing experts.

--Outside experts who emphasize one particular perspective or belief can seriously divide a movement. Not everyone in a state can or will follow any given outside expert who promotes one particular approach to education, one set of religious beliefs, moral principles, philosophy, etc. Once a minority grassroots movement has been divided, it loses the best chance it had to achieve and maintain its goals.

--Sometimes an outside expert's personal experience (for example, how he handled a similar problem in another state), training, or self-interest give him a perspective that may be inappropriate in another state or unacceptable to some members of a local organization.

RISKS OF RELYING ON CONSTITUTIONAL AND LEGAL ARGUMENTS

Some home schoolers seem to feel that the defense and protection of home schooling can be based in large part on constitutional arguments. In other words, home schoolers' rights and freedoms can best be defended by using legal arguments based in the U. S. Constitution and related case law to try to ensure that home schooling laws are reasonable and by using litigation to overcome any laws that are not. To be sure, constitutional arguments are basic and powerful. But relying primarily on them would be a serious mistake for several reasons including:

(1) Constitutional law is always subject to interpretation. Home schoolers present their interpretations, but claims and arguments made by the opposing side challenge the constitutional basis of home schooling. The courts decide who wins based on the arguments, the specifics of the case, and frankly the

117

personalities of the judges and attorneys and the socially accepted practices of the community where the case is being heard. There is no certainty as to the outcome of any given case. One hears the expression "It is the law" or "That is unconstitutional" as if there were certainty, a fixed and unbending set of rules applied uniformly in each and every case. This is not true. The words of the constitution and of statutes may be the same in a hundred cases and yet the outcomes of those cases can vary a great deal based on the facts of the case, who is arguing for and against, the judges, the place, etc.

Although constitutional principles may be familiar and generally accepted, they cannot usually be used to convince a neighbor that home schooling is acceptable or a legislator that she should vote in support of home schooling, and home schoolers need support and votes. Most people, perhaps especially legislators and the attorneys on their staffs, tend to let the courts worry about who is right about such matters as the constitutionality of a proposed legislative bill while they themselves are much more interested in why a family has chosen to home school, how it works, what it does to or for children, and how it might affect them, particularly if they owe allegiance to or are pressured by the educational establishment or are faced with voting for or against a home schooling bill.

(2) Constitutional arguments are widely used by home schoolers. If they were working well, home schooling laws and regulations throughout the United States would be much less restrictive, the good home schooling laws that do exist would not be under continual threat, and changes in the state laws would provide home schoolers with more freedom instead of fewer freedoms.

(3) Bringing an attorney, lobbyist, or expert into a legislative battle, hearing, or home schooling meeting seldom changes the need for home schoolers to take the major responsibility for themselves to protect their freedoms. They still need to know the law in their state as well as or better than the expert; to take action in the local community; to win legislators' votes; to follow up with

the educational agency responsible for administering the law to ensure that it is faithfully implemented; and to try to get regulations, forms, administrative procedures, interpretations, and even the new law changed to ensure more freedom. This is the ongoing work of home schoolers in each community and, frankly, specialists who rely on their legal expertise seldom know how to empower individuals to take charge of their own lives through grassroots organizations. Grassroots politics relies on a much broader set of facts and strategies than most attorneys possess and, in fact, relegates legal and constitutional arguments to a fairly low priority. Constitutional arguments are only one part of a grassroots effort to reclaim freedoms and maintain good laws.

In reality there are two sides to constitutional questions of law. As home schoolers we put ourselves in a very vulnerable position with regard to the law if we place a heavy reliance on the constitutional arguments for home schooling for the following reasons:

--When we look to attorneys and experts to address political issues, we do not take time to learn about the issues more clearly ourselves. We do not articulate the academic, social, psychological, moral, and logical arguments of any given issue and present these arguments to the general public, the media, relatives and neighbors, legislators, and the educational establishment.

--We fail to see that home schooling is a political act that cannot be continued without taking personal responsibility on a regular basis. We do not form effective political organizations. We do not learn the art of agreeing to disagree on certain subjects in order to be united on the basic goal that all home schoolers share and need to work together on in order to reclaim our freedoms and maintain them.

--We become complacent about our rights and learn to accept rationalizations ("The new law or regulations are the best that could be worked out.") to justify infringements on our freedoms. We do not become politically aware or responsible for our freedoms. We fail to make the connection between the structure and content of conventional schooling and the loss of personal and civil liberties and freedoms.

--We may become dependent on attorneys and other experts not just for legal questions but also for the very structure, activities, and behaviors that result from the law and determine what a home school may become or be (when the school will be in session, what types of curriculum are acceptable, whether standardized tests are required, what is needed to be an acceptable home schooler).

--We begin to expect one or a handful of self-appointed leaders or experts to solve political problems such as convincing more than half of the legislature to vote in a certain way, responding to media coverage, writing responses to local newspaper articles, talking to local school boards and school district administrators, responding to concerns of the local community, making a positive impression in each community, keeping home schoolers from offering solutions that may not be acceptable to other home schoolers, keeping home schoolers united on important questions, etc. In reality, a few leaders cannot do this and would probably create more problems than they solved if they tried to do so. We must work in our own local communities to do these things.

--It is important to be right, to have the law on our side, to interpret the law ourselves so our rights and our children's rights are protected. But being right is not enough. We also need enough power to protect ourselves and others from forces which do not operate on the basis of right and wrong.

CONCLUSION

Home schoolers must work to maintain their rights and freedom. This requires a united, grassroots effort involving all home schoolers. Simple reliance on legal arguments will not work. Instead home schoolers need to learn more about the situation in their own states (the subject of the next chapter) and decide on a course of action (the following chapter).

CHAPTER 12

LEARNING ABOUT THE POLITICS OF EDUCATION

Before you can become politically active in an effective way, you need an accurate sense of the existing situation in your local community and state. This chapter contains suggestions for determining what information you need and then gathering it.

QUESTIONS TO CONSIDER

Among the questions you may want to consider about the current situation:

(1) If your state has a home schooling law, what specifically does it require? Is this acceptable to you? Can you live with it? If not, what needs to be changed? How widespread is the problem? How much support is there for such change?

(2) Who has authority for administering the law? In other words, who is responsible for writing rules and regulations, interpreting the statutes, developing forms and procedures, and/or reviewing your home school?

(3) Who enforces the law? Is it done at the state level by the state department of education or at the local level by the school district administrator and/or the school board.

(4) Is the law strictly and uniformly enforced or does enforcement vary considerably from one local school district to another?

(5) Is any legislation pending or anticipated that is likely to impact home schoolers? Does any anticipated public school legislation offer an opportunity to reduce home schooling requirements? For example, is legislation being considered to ban standardized testing of public school students? If so, home schoolers could claim that state-mandated testing of home schoolers should be banned as well.

(6) How is educational policy determined in your state? (See pp. 131-138.)

(7) Are there any court cases pending that could impact home schoolers or home school statutes? (See pp. 144-147.)

(8) What home schooling organizations exist in your state that are effective in dealing with these questions?

(9) What positions on home schooling have been taken by key government officials (the governor, state superintendent of schools, and the leaders of the majority and minority parties in the state legislature)?

(10) Generally, is your state legislature supportive of home schooling, neutral about it, or openly opposed? Do your two state representatives support home schooling and oppose unreasonable state regulation and interference?

(11) How does the general public seem to be feeling about home schooling as reflected in conversations, media coverage, editorials, etc.?

(12) Is there anything else about the home schooling situation in your state or local community that concerns you?

POSSIBLE RESPONSES TO THE SITUATION

Once you understand the current situation, you can decide how to respond. Here are some possible responses which are discussed in detail later in this book.

(1) Accept the status quo, do nothing to try to improve the situation or prevent its worsening, and hope that the situation does not get worse for home schoolers. (This is an option, but readers of this book are by now well aware that the authors do not feel it is a very realistic approach. If you want to choose it, at least read Part VI on making the best of the current law.)

(2) Accept the status quo, do nothing active right now, read Part VI of this book on making the best of the law you have now, increase your information gathering network (see below) and be alert and ready to act should you need to.

(3) Identify a problem that needs to be solved and carefully frame the issue. (See pp. 138-140.)

(4) Try to negotiate an informal change in the enforcement of a policy that is causing difficulty. (See pp. 141-142.)

(5) Try to negotiate a change in formal policy. (See p. 142.)

(6) Work for passage of better home schooling legislation. (See pp. 143-144.)

(7) Begin the process of litigation by going to court and suing someone for something. (See pp. 144-147.)

(8) Practice civil disobedience. (See p. 148.)

(9) Develop a united, state-wide home schooling organization whose purpose is to coordinate political efforts of home schoolers. (See pp. 149-164.)

(10) Increase the number of allies and supporters you have. (See pp. 172-173.)

(11) Work more actively with the media. (See pp. 174-179.)

GETTING THE INFORMATION YOU NEED

One way to begin is by writing down as much information as you can based on what you personally know right now and think would be the best course of action for home schoolers in your state. Do it now even if you have not done anything more political than voting before. Do not wait for someone else to do it. Share the questions and your information and ideas with others, such as your spouse and/or friends and acquaintances who are home schooling. Consider discussing them in your support group. (If attendance is large at support group meetings, the group can be divided into subgroups of about 10 people who discuss the questions among themselves, then each subgroup can report to the whole group.) The initial decisions that are made will help you determine whether you need to discuss this with other home schoolers and/or what other actions you should take.

It can be very helpful to gather information in addition to that which you, your friends, and/or members of your support group know from personal experience, contacts, and reading. Gather information from other sources, such as the following. Ask each person for suggestions for other contacts.

--Other home schoolers, especially those who have been home schooling for a long time. Ask them about the history of home schooling in your state, how the current situation developed. If you have a home schooling law, ask when and why was it passed, etc.

--Legislators who have supported home schooling. Ask them how the current law came into being; whether they anticipate any home schooling bills in the near future, and if so what sort and why; and what other legislation is pending that could affect home schoolers. (See pp. 93-100 for a discussion of trends in education that affect home schoolers and pp. 241-245 for information on other laws that affect home schoolers.)

--People who are involved with small private schools. Ask them what changes have recently occurred that affect them and whether they are concerned about the possibility of changes either in legislation or in educational policy and procedures in the near future.

You can greatly expand your information and understanding of how decisions concerning education are made in your state if you enlarge your network to include people who are non-home schoolers. Valuable information from non-home schoolers can be gathered by either an informal, indirect method or a direct, formal approach.

The informal method often yields detailed and subtle information, but it generally takes longer to develop the necessary network, and it is more difficult to share or use the information directly without jeopardizing the network. This method involves developing a trust relationship with individuals in various interest groups so they feel free to share with you quasi-private information, knowing that you will use good judgment and discretion in how you use it and that they will not be hurt. Such individuals might be teachers, administrators, school board members, legislators, relatives of home schoolers, people in private schools, lobbyists in areas other than education.

The key is to recognize who is in a position to help, who is likely to help, and how to ask for their assistance, either directly or by asking someone else to get the information for you. Get perspectives from across as much of the political spectrum as possible. This is particularly crucial for a small minority like home schoolers who can ill afford to view issues solely from, for example, a Democratic or Republican perspective or from a teacher's or a businessperson's perspective. Likewise do not allow home schooling to be viewed as a partisan issue, which can happen if all your sources of information come from one political party and this becomes evident.

Through these people as well as others, such as educational lobbyists with whom you have developed a good working relationship, you can gather all kinds of information, including copies of special interest group newsletters, policy proposals, agendas for associations and their committees, evidence of conflicts among interest groups supposedly working together, surveys of legislative candidates' positions on educational proposals, and statements indicating an association's support for or opposition to particular candidates.

Other informal and indirect methods include reading newspapers, asking home schoolers and others to send you information about educational interest groups, and attending conferences where educational interests are discussed. You can also contact researchers and people on commissions that have issued reports that bear on educational interests, ask them questions, and request copies of their reports, which usually give the names and institutional affiliations of the researchers, sources, and commission members.

A more formal and direct means of gathering information is attending public legislative hearings on sensitive and important bills. Most or all of the important educational interest groups are likely to testify and be questioned by legislators. These events can be deceptive (for example, an interest group may be doing most of its lobbying with individual legislators and may prefer not to become public about a particular bill although it cares a great deal about it), but they show how these groups are aligning themselves. You are also able to learn about other organizations that have a strong interest in the bill, some of whom might become future foes or allies. You may also hear arguments and supporting information that might be used again on issues that bear more directly on home schooling.

You can ask the office of the state superintendent of instruction or the board of education to send you copies of their proposed regulations, budget estimates, testimony on a bill, supporting documentation, etc. You can also sometimes get mid-level professionals in these offices to offer opinions and attitudes about policies that lend insight into the power and interests of various educational interest groups.

You can also use your state's open records law to have sent to you copies of all correspondence, internal memorandums, documentation, and other related written information on a particular issue or topic. State government offices including public school districts are usually subject to such state laws and sometimes the federal freedom of information act. This material can yield a lot of helpful information, but your request may strain your relations with the agency or your local school district.

Other formal methods include contacting the state office responsible for maintaining a list of registered lobbyists and determining who is working for which educational groups. Also, it can be instructive to visit the state office responsible for recording campaign contributions to determine who is supporting whom and whether there is a clear pattern and resulting political indebtedness.

Written materials that may be useful:

(1) Most states publish what is called a Blue Book or Red Book, a wealth of information about legislators, their committee assignments, their affiliations, and their track records in elections. These books also describe important state offices, agencies, bureaucracies, and their budgets. In addition they include descriptions of the legislative process, rules governing bills and their passage, the text of the state constitution, and often histories of government agencies and practices. These books are generally published every two years and can be obtained by requesting one from your representative, ordering one through the legislature, or finding it in the library. However, since it takes several months after an election for the book to reflect the new legislators and committee assignments, ask your legislator for current

information or look for a special legislative supplement published in a state newspaper at the beginning of a new legislative session.

(2) Other helpful resources for developing a network and sorting out how educational policy is made include a directory of public and private schools which may include the names, addresses, and telephone numbers of administrators and a listing of professional education associations, their addresses, executive directors or presidents, and telephone numbers. There may be as many as 50 to 100 educational associations in a state, many with national affiliations. This directory will help you understand how educators are affiliated professionally, who may have a special interest in a particular bill, who is likely to be competing with others for dollars and programs, and, with time, which are the three to five associations that dominate education. You can probably find this publication through your state educational bureaucracy (ask for the publications person) or through your state representative.

(3) You may also want to obtain a listing of all legislative service agency functions and personnel as well as a directory of committee staff assignments and the aides of each representative and senator. These can be obtained through each legislative agency. Examples of such agencies are the Legislative Council, the Legislative Reference Bureau, the Legislative Fiscal or Budget Bureau, and the Legislative Audit Bureau. The directory of legislative aides is also usually available through the clerk's office in the respective legislative bodies. (In contacting legislative service agencies, be aware, that while most of them are non-partisan, they work for the legislature and their allegiance is to that body and the majority party in each body, not to the average citizen. You can get valuable information but it will be in the form of public documents and background papers. Do not expect, however, that they will do much original research, auditing, significant fact finding, etc. for you. You will need to go through your legislator and probably one or more committees to get, for example, an audit initiated.)

(4) There are also several national legislative service agencies that provide information that can be helpful in determining what is happening or about to happen with regard to educational policymaking and what is happening inside the legislatures in terms of staffing and committee and agency power. This list is not an endorsement of these agencies. They are mentioned here so that you will be aware that such agencies exist and that they can have significant influence in terms of how legislators understand issues and which ones they take up. Listed below are three such agencies.

• The National Conference of State Legislatures provides information to state legislators and their staffs including "Home Schooling: A Primer for State Legislators," January, 1989, from their series State Legislative Reports. NCSL's address is 1050 Seventeenth Street, Suite 2100, Denver, CO 80265; (303) 623-7800.

• The Council of State Governments says, "State legislators, as well as top elected and appointed state officials, are kept in touch with the trends and developments of state government through a myriad of Council publications: periodicals, research and reference books, reports, bibliographies, and occasional papers." *The Book of the States*, published every two years, will help you sort out your state government, who is doing what. (Look for it in your library.) The national headquarters address of CSG is P. O. Box 11910, Iron Works Pike, Lexington, KY 40578-9989; (606) 252-2291.

• The Education Commission of the States' primary purpose "is to help governors, state legislators, state education officials and others develop policies to improve the quality of education at all levels." This commission publishes topical materials related to educational policy and provides consulting services to policy makers. Its address is 707 17th Street, Suite 2700, Denver, CO 80202; (401) 863-1119.

HOW EDUCATIONAL POLICY IS DETERMINED

Understanding how educational policy is made in your state will enable you to create a more positive climate for home schooling. First, such knowledge will make you more effective in dealing with the principal educational forces of your state. Second, it will better enable you to anticipate the ramifications and repercussions of policy initiatives and know what to say and what to do about them.

There are at least three key factors to consider in determining how educational policy is made in your state. These are, first, how public education is funded in your state; second, how your state superintendent is selected; and, third, the relative strength and relationship among the principal players in educational policymaking.

FUNDING FOR EDUCATION

Much of educational public policy is decided on the basis of money. Many more decisions are based on what an educational program will cost, who will make money from it, and who will have to pay for it than on whether the program is likely to result in learning or benefit students. (Related to the question of money is loss of jobs in education or loss of professional status due to alternative non-public school programs.) The people participating most directly in educational decisions will vary from state to state depending on how education is funded. In California, public education is financed by state-wide taxes rather than local property taxes and therefore funding decisions tend to be made exclusively by the state legislature. In New Hampshire, local district taxes (as distinct from state-wide taxes) account for virtually the entire financial base of public schools, and funding decisions are made by people attending town meetings. It is no surprise that California has been one of the states which has mandated which textbook will be used by grade and subject for every school in the state while in New Hampshire such decisions are made primarily at the local level.

Most states combine state-wide taxes with local taxes to fund public education. In any case in most states, public elementary and secondary education accounts for over half the combined local and state budgets, and education costs have gone up significantly over the past ten years. Some state constitutions limit how much the state is able to spend through state revenues on public education.

Recognizing differences in how education is funded will help you understand how educational policy decisions are made. For example in states where a large percentage of the funding comes through state-wide taxes, you will probably find strong state-wide associations and lobbying efforts by teachers unions, local public school administrators, local school boards, business interests, and state officials. You may also find the legislatures in such states more active in mandating programs and making requirements of public schools in exchange for increased state expenditures to schools. In states that rely almost exclusively on local taxes, there are likely to be fewer state-mandated programs and less power exerted by educational interest groups.

SELECTION OF STATE SUPERINTENDENT

A second major factor in determining how decisions affecting education are made in your state is how key state level education officials are selected and to whom they report or are held accountable. The top state level public school official in each state is placed in office either by direct election or by appointment. There are a variety of ways in which this is done.

Thirty five states plus the District of Columbia have appointed superintendents. In 14 of these states (AK, AR, CT, DE, IL, MD, MA, MO, NH, RI, SD, TX, VT, and WV), the governor appoints a state board of education and the board members appoint the state superintendent. In 12 states (AL, CO, DC, HI, KS, LA, MI, NE, NV, NM, OH, and UT) the board is elected and then appoints the superintendent. In seven states (IA, ME, MN, NJ, PA, TN, and VA), the governor appoints both the board and the

132

superintendent. In New York the legislature selects the board which then appoints the superintendent. In Mississippi, a board appointed by the governor, lieutenant governor, and the speaker of the legislature appoints the superintendent.

Sixteen states elect their superintendents. In 12 states (AZ, CA, GA, ID, IN, KY, MT, NC, ND, OK, OR, and WY), a board of education is appointed by the governor but the superintendent is elected. In Florida, both the board and the superintendent are elected. In Washington, local boards select a board and the superintendent is elected. In South Carolina, the legislature selects the board and the superintendent is elected. Finally, Wisconsin is the only state without a state board; the superintendent is elected.

In general the state boards of education perform administrative and regulatory functions and have legal authority to govern local schools. An important point to keep in mind is that although these boards were often created to insulate educational policymaking from the political process, such policy-making is highly political and the boards in reality seldom have much direct policymaking power. Such power resides primarily with the legislature and its staffs and to a lesser degree with the state superintendent. The state superintendent's power will vary according to how she is selected. The selection process in turn helps determine which special interest groups (such as teachers unions, associations of local administrators, local school boards, business associations, etc.) are most able to affect this selection. Once in office the superintendent's actions are likely to reflect the interests of the people who were most influential in selecting her, and her ability to advance these interests will be much greater if these same interests are also strong in the legislature.

INTERACTION OF KEY PLAYERS

A third major factor influencing how decisions concerning education are made is the relative strength and relationship between the principal players in educational policymaking. This

133

includes teachers, local administrators, local school boards, private schools, the state university system, state educational officials, members of education committees in the legislature, the state association of manufacturers and commerce, the media, and the general public.

Rarely will any single interest group dominate educational public policy to such an extent that this group is able consistently to get the bills it supports passed by the legislature. At the same time there are no formal checks and balances within the educational sector of our society, and thus there are no hard and fast divisions between interest groups. These two realities mean that the educational interest groups need each other to get their bills passed in the legislature. They create informal temporary coalitions around pieces of legislation. The alignments will vary depending somewhat on the subject of the legislation but primarily on who holds power in the legislature and how they were elected.

For example, the state association of local school district administrators might be aligned quite consistently with the teachers union in a state where the teachers union is quite influential in electing legislators. This will be true for several reasons. First, although administrators often oppose teachers on questions of salary, benefits, and professional status, administrators also share many objectives with teachers such as larger budgets and programs to serve their schools. Second, among the primary educational interest groups, administrators are the ones perhaps most in need of allies since there are so few of them relative to teachers or local school board members. Also, unlike most school board members, they view their positions as career positions and are therefore less likely to take political risks. Third, if teachers in this example are quite influential in electing legislators, they probably have also been able to establish a strong union position that already limits the administrators' management options. Fourth, the teachers may also have played a large role in selecting the state superintendent. (This may not be true for example in a state where the governor appoints the superintendent and the governor is of a different party from the majority party of the legislature.) In a different state the administrators might align with a business association and/or the school boards over against the teachers if these interest groups hold more power in the legislature and in selecting the state superintendent.

In terms of the relative strengths of these educational interest groups, the teachers represent the largest single professional group and far outnumber most special interest groups both in and out of the educational arena. In states where they are well organized, their lobbying efforts are quite effective. Their power is more than just numbers and large legislative budgets. Their numbers are evenly distributed throughout legislative districts. Teachers tend to be more verbal and articulate than the average citizen and are trained to take political action. They hold considerable interpersonal power over citizens because education is still highly valued and because teachers can make it difficult for the children of families that oppose positions supported by teachers.

Business interests are perhaps the only organized opposition that comes close to challenging well organized teachers. Such challenges come almost exclusively in terms of funding questions rather than programmatic or policy questions. Businesses may be critical of public schools and teachers unions in general terms, but basically they want the schools to produce a work force prepared to advance business interests and therefore wish to remain partners with the public schools. Businesses will work to keep education expenditures low but seldom will lobby overtly or publicly against public school programs or teachers.

Local school boards have lost a lot of their political power during the past 30 years as schools have been consolidated, legislatures have assumed larger roles in financing and directing schools, and local administrators have acquired more power through multi-million dollar budgets and large staffs and facilities. One of the consequences is that the average tenure of a local school board member is now only one year. This does not allow for much institutional memory or power relative to teachers, and often the school board is nearly a rubber stamp for the local administrator's decisions and agenda. Yet, most school boards still do have the legal authority to control budgets, hire and fire people, determine programs, establish policy, enforce the compulsory school attendance laws, and generally direct the local public school.

The state university system represents another strong force in educational policymaking. Yet, the system itself seldom takes a public stand on sensitive policy questions related to public elementary and secondary schools. There are two primary reasons for this. First, in most states the state university budget and the state budget for elementary and secondary schools are strongly interrelated if not joined and voted on as one. There tends to be a target figure of dollars for education as a whole and criticisms or suggestions for reductions in the elementary and secondary schools could mean a smaller pie to be divided between higher education and the local public schools or could lead to reciprocal criticisms and hence fewer dollars for everybody. Second, the system represents the source of a lot of the teacher training and practices used by public schools and would be create a lot of change within its own system if it voiced and endorsed the criticisms and studies by researchers that show the inadequacies of conventional schools. For example, in 1986 the Carnegie Forum on Education and the Economy published a report entitled *A Nation Prepared: Teachers for the 21st Century* which recommended abolishing undergraduate degrees in teacher education. Imagine what adopting such a policy would do to the budgets and facilities of most state university systems.

Although the media has reported on hundreds of critical commission studies, public opinion surveys, and recommendations for educational reform, it tends nevertheless to accept rather than question or challenge public school spokespersons. When the media feels it necessary to provide "balanced" reporting in education, it finds an opposing special interest advocate and paraphrases or quotes this person. Little if any investigative reporting about education is done. As with the business sector, the media is usually careful not to challenge public education directly and concretely at the state or local level.

The general public gets most of its information about education from the media rather than directly from schools for two reasons. First, only 25% of today's adult population has school age children. Second, the larger schools of today with their standardized, routinized, and specialized approaches to education have evolved so that a teacher's feedback to a parent is generally through impersonal test scores. According to recent Gallop poll surveys, many teachers and principals do not welcome or want substantive parental participation in a child's public school education. The public school system has in effect defined parents as extraneous to a child's education, and there is little communication between parent and school personnel. (All the special public relations efforts and special programs to involve parents in education are not really designed to change the system. Although professional educators and their standardized practices cannot be shown to correlate with learning and only family background and parental participation do consistently correlate with learning (see p. 99), public school officials argue that it is parents who need to change, not the school system. The educational establishment is blaming parents and proposing that the educational system educate parents on how to be effective parents which means convincing them to accept and support the system's needs.)

Whether it is money, the selection of a state superintendent, or how education interest groups are aligned, it is important to understand how public policy concerning education is being made in your state. You can use this knowledge in (1) framing issues, (2) finding allies, (3) working for or against bills impacting home schoolers, (4) timing your responses, (5) getting others to make your case for you, (6) deciding what arguments and supporting information to use, and (7) working with the media. For example, if your state requires standardized testing of home schoolers and is about to consider banning the use of standardized testing in the elementary grades of public schools, you could anticipate the ramifications of this proposal and devise ways of

137

ensuring that it works for home schoolers rather than against them. It could work for home schoolers if it led to the removal of required standardized testing of home schoolers. It could work against home schoolers if it led to replacing standardized tests with a more demanding requirement. Knowing how this policy is regarded by those who are most powerful in determining funding decisions, what the state superintendent's position is on the topic, and the relative strengths and alignments of educational interest groups on the issue should help you to make effective decisions and deal with such an issue long before it becomes a law that affects home schoolers.

FRAMING THE ISSUE

Framing the issue is one of the most important parts of any effort to accomplish a goal or make a change. The way you describe and present the problem and proposed solutions will have a strong effect on the reaction of allies, neutral parties, and opponents. A clear statement of purpose and plan of action will do a lot to organize, motivate, and give direction to the people with whom you are working. Defining the issue broadly so you demonstrate to many people that they should be concerned can win new allies. A strong, well-reasoned statement may weaken, deflate, or demoralize your adversaries.

How an issue or question is stated and understood can determine much about how it gets resolved. For example, in Wisconsin the educational establishment framed their desire to control home schoolers in terms of the need to change the compulsory school attendance law so it could be enforced. They focused on the legal issue of constitutionality rather on making the case that a reasonable law to regulate home schoolers was needed. After a long fight during which major changes favorable to home schoolers were made to their bill, the establishment not only had lost the bill they wanted but were now unable to get the governor to veto the bill since the press had reported for months that Wisconsin was the only state in the nation without a compulsory school attendance law.

138

Another example comes from a bill in the U. S. Congress to provide federal money to a national board on teacher certification. There were several ways to frame the issue. Unfortunately some home schoolers allowed the issue to be framed in terms of what this bill would or might do to home schoolers; rumors spread that it would require certification of home schoolers. This caused problems for several reasons. First, the bill had nothing directly to do with home schoolers. Second, the issue of money was less important than the precedent of the federal government's supporting an educational interest group and thereby granting it status and endorsing its certification philosophy. Third, home schoolers' concerns were addressed by a clarifying amendment stating that the bill was not intended to affect them. This had no effect on the serious questions raised by the bill and did not resolve its problems. Fourth, home schoolers who expressed concern about an imagined threat could be seen as not knowing what they were talking about.

The issue could have been framed in terms of the inappropriateness of the federal government's assisting a private entity to attain greater professional standing or in terms of problems with the federal government's supporting a move to nationalize what is now a state responsibility, that is, the certification of teachers. Then home schoolers could have worked against the bill on grounds that would have educated Congress regarding alternatives to certification and the need to move away from specialization in education. This might have served home schoolers' long-term interests much better than a somewhat meaningless amendment, an embarrassing first major showing by home schoolers with the U. S. Congress.

Framing the issue is an on-going process that can take many forms. Perhaps a small group of people work together to define the real problem and develop a plan for action. This may then be written as an issue paper and presented to a larger group, the membership of an organization, the general public, etc. Further refinement of the issue occurs as people continue to meet, discuss, and act; as additional information and new developments are reported in newsletters; and as fact sheets and white papers are prepared for distribution to legislators and potential supporters. Keeping the real issue uppermost in people's mind does a great deal to empower a movement, center and focus it, and keep it on track.

Different kinds of statements work for different groups. Much time and energy can be saved if someone drafts an options paper before a planning meeting. This can include a tentative statement of the problem or issue, which the group may then modify or completely rewrite, plus a list of alternative actions. Even if the group ends up with a completely different set of goals and plans than those presented in the original options paper, it still provided a point of departure to get the discussion going.

Statements for newsletters and fact sheets benefit from both a strong summary at the beginning and specific details to support the arguments. The importance of including as much pertinent information as possible has to be balanced with the fact that shorter statements are less expensive to print and more likely to be read. Sometimes it works well to write a rough draft stating exactly what you think and feel, using language as strong as you want, and then revise it, if necessary, so it is more likely to gain support. As you write, keep asking yourself what the most important points are. Sometimes a question and answer format works well, especially when providing information for other home schoolers who will then be presenting it to legislators, school boards, etc. You can anticipate likely questions and provide suggested responses to help members prepare for their presentations or conversations.

Framing the issue takes time and careful thought, but it is very important. When Pat Montgomery says, "I encourage homeschoolers to realize how what they're doing fits in the broad scheme of resurrecting the family as a pillar of society," (*Home Education Magazine*, Vol. 7 No. 5, Sept/Oct, 1990, p. 16), she is framing an issue; empowering home schoolers; attracting the attention of potential allies; and giving life, energy, and focus to the home schooling movement.

140

CHAPTER 13

OPTIONS FOR CHANGING
EDUCATIONAL POLICY

On the basis of information gathered (using suggestions from the preceding chapter or by other means), home schoolers often conclude that an educational policy that affects them needs to be changed. Different approaches can be used. This chapter will discuss negotiation, legislation, litigation, referendum initiative, and civil disobedience.

NEGOTIATING INFORMAL CHANGE

Changes can be made informally by convincing people who administer a law to use one interpretation of that law rather than another or by getting them to act or not act on specific issues. In other words, there may be instances where all parties informally agree to disregard the ambiguity of a statute and by doing so in effect change policy by allowing existing or preferred practice to proceed without a clear and formal policy in writing. School administrators and other public officials are accustomed to having people obey their pronouncements. They are often so surprised to be countered by a reasonable home schooler who clearly knows what her legal rights are and is making a reasonable request that they are more willing than might be expected to negotiate a solution to a problem. It is important for home schoolers to know what is going on and what their rights are and to confront officials in situations that can be resolved in this way. This has happened when home schoolers have requested that their child be allowed to take driver education from a public school. At first the administrator said no and claimed that this was the policy, but when the parent persisted and showed that the state reimbursed a school district under such circumstances, the child was able to take the class.

NEGOTIATING POLICY CHANGE

Sometimes change can be quickly, easily, and inexpensively accomplished by negotiating with a public official who has authority to alter the policy in question. Home schoolers can prepare to meet with the official by having clearly in mind exactly what change they want, what arguments support their request, how they could counter objections the official is likely to have to their request, how they will respond to other alternatives the official may offer, and what they will do if the official refuses. Non-home schoolers who support the request can be included. Common courtesy should be used regardless of the official's response, and care is needed to be sure an even less desirable alternative is not proposed by the official and then accepted.

An example of the successful application of this approach occurred in Wisconsin in 1984. The Department of Public Instruction (DPI) overstepped its authority by including more on the required form for home schoolers than the newly passed law allowed. Home schoolers planned together. Then a representative of Wisconsin Parents Association, the leader of an association of small private schools, and legislators who had been key supporters of the law met with a DPI official to explain the problem. As a result of the meeting, the DPI changed the form to conform with the law. The use of negotiation avoided the need for a lawsuit, civil disobedience (had home schoolers refused to turn in the form, which is required by law), and an illegal and unreasonable increase by the DPI in its power, authority, and regulation over home schoolers. Had home schoolers not protested, they would have lost part of their freedom and rights.

142

LEGISLATION

Having the state legislature pass a fair and reasonable home schooling law may seem at first glance like an excellent goal for home schoolers. However, there are important advantages to <u>not</u> having any home schooling law at all, if that is possible. (See pp. 216-218.) Also, before undertaking a campaign for a new law, home schoolers should carefully consider the pitfalls and risks, which include the following.

--It is difficult to gather a strong enough constituency to get a home schooling law through a state legislature. Minorities fare much better working to defeat legislation rather than trying to get it passed. Home schoolers comprise less than one per cent of the school aged population, and parents of school aged children represent only 25% of the adult population in America today. There is not a large natural constituency for home schooling. Rather this constituency needs to be built, and a good way is in response to an injustice being perpetrated on home schoolers or in support of home schoolers as underdogs in a fight they did not start. Seldom can home schoolers initiate the fight and at the same time establish legislation or regulations that increase their freedom to home school. Allies and supporters can be found (see pp. 172-173), but minorities face an uphill battle in trying to get legislation passed, even if they do not have the strong opposition that home schoolers face in most states (see pp. 91-93). Another major problem is that in many states one (or more) of the legislature's education committees is controlled by the educational establishment. Although this committee cannot always get its bills passed, it can certainly prevent bills relating to education from reaching the full legislature. In such situations the only reasonable way to get a bill passed is to attach it to a budget bill or get the bill assigned to a committee that would not normally deal with education bills.

--Once a bill has been introduced, it can be completely changed by amendment any time during the legislative process. A bill introduced to support one side of an issue can be amended so it ends up supporting the opposite side. For example,

Wisconsin's current reasonable home schooling law was originally introduced by the educational establishment as a bill that would have severely regulated home schooling. Home schoolers who have a favorable bill introduced for them are giving their adversaries a golden opportunity, and they should be sure they can control or defeat such opposition before requesting or supporting the introduction of any home schooling legislation.

--Home schoolers are a diverse group of people who have different reasons for home schooling and varied approaches to education. Getting home schoolers to agree on what would be a reasonable home schooling law would be difficult and could divide home schoolers and provide a good opportunity for opponents of home schooling.

Therefore, home schoolers would generally be wise to confine their legislative activity to preventing passage of unreasonable legislation which someone else has initiated. Occasionally home schoolers can succeed in turning such legislative threats into good home schooling laws, so such situations should be considered carefully to see what opportunities, if any, they provide. Nevertheless, home schoolers' best legislative strategy is generally a defensive reaction. When asked to propose legislation or to provide examples of legislation that would be acceptable, home schoolers' best response is usually that state regulation of home schools is unnecessary and would be harmful. Also, it is generally wise to live with minor problems or ambiguous language in the statutes rather than to allow the statute to be introduced for amendment in the legislature.

LITIGATION

Another way to deal with an unreasonable law (or regulation or administrative policy) is by means of a lawsuit in which the court is asked to overturn a law or rule in one's favor because the law, regulation, or policy is unconstitutional or violates some other statute or principle of law. This tempting alternative has several serious pitfalls.

--Court cases are often long, very costly, usually require trained legal help to handle logistics and technicalities, and have very serious outcomes. It is better not to initiate a court case than to present one poorly and lose. Serious consideration should be given to questions such as: Do we have the resources necessary to handle this case well? Is this the best use of our limited resources of time, energy, and money? Is there any other way this question or difficulty could be resolved? Do we have a reasonable chance of success? Will winning the case prompt new unfavorable home schooling legislation and, if so, will home schoolers be able to defeat such legislation?

--It is difficult to have a law ruled unconstitutional. There is generally a strong presumption of constitutionality in any law passed by a legislature. It may be especially difficult to have a home schooling law declared unconstitutional on religious grounds. First, as a result of recent home schooling legislation, most laws make specific provisions for freedom of religion. Second, when the constitutionality of laws relating to home schooling has been challenged, the litigation has often concerned questions of whether existing statutes (1) defined compulsory school attendance and/or private schools and/or home schools clearly enough, (2) could require private and home schools to be substantially equivalent to public schools, (3) could require that instructors in home schools and private schools be certified or otherwise have the credentials required of public school teachers, and/or (4) were consistent with other constitutional provisions. Generally the successful challenges by home schoolers have been argued on the basis of vagueness (number one above) and not on the basis of religion.

Very few cases have been won on the basis of freedom of religion or religious liberty. The 1972 U.S. Supreme Court case *Yoder v. Wisconsin* is sometimes cited. However, although there are encouraging sentences about the importance of parental participation in religious training and practice, the court provided an exemption from the compulsory school attendance law based on several demanding considerations: (1) the people involved have been practicing a separatist religion for centuries, (2) the children are highly unlikely to be seeking to participate in mainstream American society, (3) their religious beliefs and practices require that children not attend high school, and (4) the children are highly unlikely to become burdens on society. Few if any other people are likely to meet such rigorous criteria for exemption from the compulsory school attendance law, so this would be a very limited precedent for home schoolers to try to use.

--A case may become a pawn of more powerful individuals or institutions that have a very different agenda. This is a risk especially for people who have gotten involved in a case to prove a point. Sometime their efforts backfire as the issue for which they were fighting is lost or becomes distorted or is used to support an end very different from the one they envisioned.

--Litigation often leads to legislation as opponents of home schooling take advantage of the opening provided by a court case to propose new home schooling legislation or regulation.

If either a supporter or an opponent of home schooling initiates a court case, the following should be considered:

--Track any litigation that might impact on home schooling laws. View the case from your perspective as a resident of your state, even if the case is being handled by attorneys experienced dealing with home schooling laws. You can remain neutral as far as the case itself goes. But if you want to be involved and support one side, consider offering either suggestions and arguments or acting as an amicus curiae. On the other hand, if the case is causing serious problems, put as much distance as possible between it and the vast majority of home schoolers in the state.

--Inform home schoolers in your state about the nature of the case, what the outcome might be, what results might follow, and how they can prepare for the possible outcome. Consider legislative changes that might result from the litigation and whether they are preferable to existing law. Prepare to support positive legislation and defeat unfavorable legislation if necessary.

--If your state does not already have a united state-wide, inclusive home schooling organization, consider forming one while the case is still in progress. Do not wait for the results because you may not have enough time to organize and act then. Also, similar legal disputes may follow that also require a political organization within the state.

REFERENDUM INITIATIVE

The referendum initiative is available in many states and is something to consider. It allows for circumventing the legislative process and thereby avoiding the powerful educational establishment's control over many facets of public policy in the legislature. But there are three main difficulties with using this mechanism to gain better statutes or policies for home schooling. First, it will be difficult to gain support of the general public or out lobby or out spend the educational establishment in educating people and winning their support. This obstacle may sometimes be overcome or lessened if such an effort is combined with a larger parental rights issue or an initiative on choice in education. Second, it is highly likely that if you are to gain any substantive advantage, especially any monetary benefit for home schooling, you will need to demonstrate that you are willing to accept significant regulation in order to be successful with the referendum. Serious consideration must be given to the question of whether the money is really worth the loss of freedom. Third, the educational establishment can always change your statute or policy through the legislative process or its own referendum. However, despite the difficulties associated with referendums, they nevertheless may represent a better alternative for change than either legislation or litigation.

CIVIL DISOBEDIENCE

Deliberately and self-consciously refusing to obey an unfair law and accepting consequences such as a fine or imprisonment are not common responses to unreasonable home schooling laws at this time, but they are alternatives home schoolers could consider. This might be particularly effective if home schoolers were united in their position, if there was no significant evidence that the policy was needed or effective in terms of ensuring that children did not grow up to be a burden on the state, and if home schoolers from all walks of life were willing to pay the consequences of their disobedience and found ways to publicize what was happening and why it was happening. What would happen if home schoolers refused to have their children take state-mandated standardized tests, for example?

CONCLUSION

Home schoolers who feel a change is needed in an unreasonable home schooling law or regulation have a variety of options available to them. Generally negotiating a change is the best alternative, although it does not always work. Legislation and litigation are other approaches, but they each have serious potential problems. Referendum initiatives offer an interesting option in states where they are available. Civil disobedience is also a possibility. While home schoolers are working to bring about change, or should change prove impossible, they need to deal with the current situation. For suggestions, see Part VI, Making the Best of Current Law.

CHAPTER 14

GRASSROOTS HOME SCHOOLING ORGANIZATIONS

A strong grassroots organization that welcomes and unites the home schoolers in a state is one of the most important assets home schoolers can have. This chapter provides background and suggestions for developing and maintaining such an organization. The more clearly the principles and foundations of the organization are understood by those participating in it, the stronger the organization will be.

THE PURPOSE OF THE ORGANIZATION

At first glance it may seem difficult to envision an organization of home schoolers. A wide range of people choose to home school for a variety of reasons and in different ways. The process of getting these diverse people to agree on anything and work together may seem mind-boggling. There is, however, a good way of resolving this dilemma. The one point on which virtually all home schoolers can agree is the need to exercise their right to home school without undue intervention and regulation from the state. A strong, viable organization can be based on this purpose and the agreement that all other home schooling concerns are the responsibility of each individual family.

The statement of purpose of such an organization could include the following:

149

--The purpose of the organization is to reclaim, preserve, protect, and defend the right of parents to home school their children without undue interference or regulation by the state. This could also be expressed in terms of parents' right to secure for their children an education consistent with their beliefs and principles, which of course would include home schooling.

--The organization will achieve its purpose by (1) monitoring and reviewing state policy relating to home schooling at all levels from state law to administrative code to policy application, (2) monitoring any litigation that might impact on home schools, and (3) empowering individuals to take effective political action. It will develop an organizational network throughout the state to enable home schoolers to work together and support each other in achieving this purpose. It will communicate with its members through a regular newsletter and special bulletins as needed. It may hold workshops in local areas and/or an annual state-wide conference. It will encourage its members to become politically active, including communicating with their legislators, and will supply them with information to assist them.

--The organization will take no position or stand on questions relating to approaches to education, methods of teaching, curriculums, or religious or philosophical beliefs and ideas. It will welcome all home schoolers and not require that they take any particular position on these questions. There are two main reasons for this. First is the practical consideration that as a small minority, home schoolers can maximize their strength in dealing with adversaries and with the legislature only if they remain united. If they split and disagree among themselves over matters such as individual principles and beliefs or approaches to education, they seriously weaken their effect. Second, each family must decide for itself what is most important and works best when it comes to the specifics of conducting a home school. It is important to realize that this strategy of not taking a position on these issues and beliefs works very well for a home schooling organization because parents can be trusted to educate their own children, because state regulation of home schooling is unnecessary and may be harmful, and because home schooling works because it has the flexibility to meet the needs of individual children.

--The organization will not get involved in any cause except home schooling. Many of the members will no doubt be active in supporting a variety of other causes, but organizational involvement with any other cause, however worthwhile, will inevitably weaken and possibly divide the organization. For the same reason, the organization will not formally endorse or support any political candidate.

--The organization will work to empower its members so they can work individually and together to protect their rights.

--The organization will rely on the abilities, experience, commitment, and history of its members and not on outside experts. (For more information on the importance of this, see pp. 116-117.)

--Of course some home schoolers are interested in a group that is involved in other activities in addition to political action. They also want a chance to share their positive feelings and their concerns about home schooling with others who agree with their approaches, principles, and beliefs. These needs are better met by small local support groups which can gather frequently and in which people can get to know each other. The state organization can encourage the formation of such local support groups by helping home schoolers who live in the same area get in touch with each other (with the home schoolers' permission).

LAUNCHING THE ORGANIZATION

It is generally easier to bring people together and get them organized and committed if there is a crisis or a clear and present danger (such as the introduction of home schooling legislation) and/or if the proposed organization articulates a goal that will strongly interest people or provides a needed service.

151

You can begin by seeking out and solidifying a core group of like-minded people who agree on basic principles, if not specific approaches. It may be helpful to develop an issue paper or some other concrete means of communicating and working out issues, questions, and concerns among the people who already share such questions. You can include in the issue paper your ideas for the purposes and goals of the organization (some of the phrases and ideas from the above discussion may be helpful here). Then the core group can add to and modify them. You can also include a tentative list of proposed activities, and the group can decide which will be undertaken immediately, who will take responsibility for each of them, and which will be given serious consideration for the future. The following are activities such an organization may want to undertake. (More detailed suggestions for some of them are found in other sections of this book. For more ideas on issue papers, see pp. 138-140.)

--Review developing state policy that might impact home schooling at all levels from legislative bills to state law to administrative code and regulations.

--Track issues related to education in the legislature and related state agencies. (It is more helpful to use a personal network to gather information about potential legislation and its significance and likelihood of support and passage than to rely on a computerized list of new legislation that does not answer key questions such as why the bill is being introduced, how strong support for the bill is, and what the best response is.)

--Lobby for home schooling interests in the state legislature.

--Organize contacts with legislators so that each legislator is contacted by home schoolers in his or her district.

--Develop an organizational network throughout the state, linking support groups and individual home schoolers into a functioning unit that can respond when necessary to legislative issues, etc. This may include a telephone tree.

--Publish a regular newsletter.

--Issue special bulletins as needed.

--Hold workshops at various points throughout the state.

--Have an annual state-wide conference.

SETTING UP AN ORGANIZATIONAL STRUCTURE

Fit the organizational structure, style, and image of the organization to its purpose and goals. (Short term or long term? With approximately how many members?) With a fledgling volunteer organization, it sometimes works well to fit the structure to the available personnel and allow flexibility for change as the organization grows and develops. As it becomes larger, a more formal structure may be helpful. One common approach is to have a board of directors or council from whom are selected people who assume such roles as president, executive director, recording and corresponding secretaries, and treasurer. People may also serve as legislative liaison or coordinator, conference coordinator, newsletter writer/editor, mailing list coordinator, telephone tree coordinator, etc.; these people may or may not be members of the board or council.

In the interest of good will and long-term cooperation, it often works well to run the board by consensus (everyone is willing to agree to a proposal or at least no one feels strongly enough about it to oppose it) rather than by majority rule. However, it can be helpful to have by-laws to fall back on should problems and disagreements arise.   Generally by-laws should be straightforward, basic, and not too detailed. Avoid getting bogged down in long discussions over legal technicalities or highly unlikely hypothetical situations. It is also a good idea to have board meetings open to all members of the organization (with the option that the board can meet in executive session if necessary) and to distribute minutes of the meetings to board members.

The state can be divided into regions, by counties or in some other convenient way. Each is served by a regional coordinator, who may or may not be a member of the board but who communicates regularly with the board or the president or executive director. Regional coordinators are an important link between the board and the members. They can help local support groups get started and coordinate efforts of members dealing with local issues and with the legislators from that region. It should be made clear, however, that regional coordinators are not support group leaders (although the same person could serve in both functions if she had enough time and energy). A regional coordinator acts according to the unifying purpose of the organization and does not take a position or stand on questions of personal principles and beliefs or approaches to education, whereas a support group leader may want to take a position on these subjects since the group itself may be based on one or more of such personal principles and beliefs.

Criteria used to select a regional coordinator might include: 1. good speaking and writing skills; 2. organizational skills (such as ability to get information out to and back from individuals and organizations in an efficient manner and to structure, implement, and operate a phone tree); 3. skills in interpersonal relationships and group dynamics (ability to listen to and communicate with a wide variety of people, including those who may not have similar values and lifestyles, and ability to negotiate or arbitrate differences of opinion); 4. commitment to home schooling and ability to adjust one's own personal position for the sake of a larger group's objective or goal; 5. use of good judgment in handling delicate personal and political issues and questions and knowing when to ask for assistance; 6. willingness to commit several hours a month to carrying out the regional coordinator's job; and 7. interest in issues and events related to home schooling.

--It should be emphasized that such an organization will be most effective if its officers, board members, regional coordinators, and the general membership understand that their involvement with the organization is to ensure that its purpose is fulfilled and not to represent, protect, advocate, or otherwise advance a specific approach to education, a specific reason for home schooling, or a specific belief system. These concerns can best be dealt with in local support groups as distinct from a state-wide grassroots political organization.

GENERAL PRINCIPLES FOR SUSTAINING AN ORGANIZATION

--Include as many people in leadership roles as possible without threatening the organization's principles and objectives. Develop relatively clear roles and authorities for people in the organization.

--Be as predictable and "professional" as possible relative to your members. Do not extend the same courtesy to your adversaries, however; sometimes the element of surprise works very well in your favor.

--Anticipate upcoming issues and problems. Try to stay one or two steps ahead of most people's concerns and the need for action. This can be done by having an effective network of active grassroots members who pick up issues long before they become widely known in the state capitol or in the media.

--Do not assume a new volunteer will understand clearly how things should be done or will be reliable. Talk regularly with people who have important responsibilities until it is clear that they understand and are following through.

--It often works well for the leaders of a grassroots organization representing a minority to maintain a low profile or even be anonymous. (For example, a newsletter may list regional coordinators but not the authors of the newsletter or the officers of the organization.) This helps the members understand that it is their work and their responsibility and helps to avoid the "big person" syndrome where people expect the leaders to take care of everything. It ensures that members are given credit for work that they do and keeps the leaders honest. It also makes the movement appear larger and deeper and keeps the opposition guessing about who and what the organization really is, so the element of surprise is retained. This also means legislators, who are accustomed to dealing with paid lobbyists who purport to speak for large numbers of people, cannot say, "Well I spoke with the home schoolers' person (or lobbyist), and he said...." There is an enormous political difference between a leader or lobbyist speaking for all of General Electric or a state's affiliate of the National Education Association (NEA) and a leader or lobbyist speaking for home schoolers. We need to make our voice much larger than our numbers or dollars, and we can do this if we win over people in our communities and have them join in our voices.

--In a grassroots organization, the members assume responsibility for work that needs to be done and do it themselves rather than relying on the leadership of the organization to do everything. However, this does not mean there is no leadership. A grassroots organization is not necessarily a democracy. Sometimes the complexity of a situation or the need for quick action means that the leadership has to make decisions and act on them without consulting the full membership. However, the leader (the president, executive director, or the person responsible for the issue) should consult with board members before acting, unless this is absolutely impossible. Taking time to make careful decisions by consensus pays big dividends in the long run, especially when the organization has anticipated and prepared for problems in advance of a crisis.

--Members of a grassroots organization share with leaders the responsibility for maintaining an appropriate balance between the work of the leadership and that of the members. The following questions may be helpful for members who need to ask whether they should be following the current leaders or pressing for change in leaders or in the way decisions are made and work done. The questions may be helpful to leaders as well.

(1)   Are you getting accurate and complete information concerning issues your organization is facing and policies by which it operates or do you feel left in the dark about important matters?

(2) Are you being asked to take an active role in determining outcomes or are you being asked to leave key outcomes to the leaders and not rock the boat?

(3)   If the leaders decide the organization should not participate in a given activity, are good reasons given for such a refusal?

(4) Are all individuals given credit for successes or do the leaders take credit largely for themselves?

(5) Do you feel empowered by your participation in the organization and better able to manage your own life as a result or do you feel dependent on the organization and its leaders?

(6) Do the leaders work primarily for the benefit of the organization or do they gain significantly in personal status, money, or power by their actions?

(7) As a result of your membership in the organization, have you done something concrete that made a difference? If not, has the organization helped you obtain the opportunity, resources, and encouragement to do something that made a difference?

(8) Do you have the sense that the members of the organization really make the difference, or is it primarily the leaders who are getting things done?

(9) Does the organization encourage people to work from strength, self-confidence, and positive purposes or does it rely on fears and insecurities?

--Members who express concern and/or criticism can be invited to the next board meeting, unless the issues they raise need more urgent attention.

FUNDING

Annual membership dues are a good source of income. Be sure to point out the benefits of membership, which can include subscription to the newsletter, a discount on conference registration fees and materials the organization publishes, and most importantly the benefits that come from participating in a grassroots organization that is actively working to empower its members so they can work together to protect their rights.

A well run conference can be a good source of income; see below for suggestions. Sometimes donations can be secured from businesses and foundations. One complication, however, stems from the fact that many such groups only make contributions to non-profit, tax-exempt organizations, and to obtain this designation from the IRS, you need to limit significantly your lobbying activity. Also, remember that when you accept money from an individual or an organization, you are at least informally linking the organization to the benefactor. Consider seriously whether this association could hurt your cause, now or in the future.

NEWSLETTERS

A newsletter can be a tremendous asset for a grassroots organization. Among the functions it can serve are:

(1) A newsletter can inform members about current issues and concerns and help them prepare for possible future crises. One of the most important functions a newsletter can perform is to provide background information, explanations of how things work, and suggestions for ways in which members could respond if a problem arises.

(2) A newsletter projects an image of an organization and a message about it. A neat, attractive, readable newsletter with timely and accurate information says to members that the organization is healthy and functioning well and will support and back them up as they carry out their work. It says to adversaries

that you are well organized and a force to be reckoned with. And it says to potential supporters and allies that the organization has its act together and is trustworthy and deserving of support.

In writing and editing the newsletter, you may want to keep the following ideas in mind. (Please remember that these apply to newsletters published by state-wide grassroots political organizations. Many support groups prefer to publish much warmer, friendlier, more practical newsletters with first person stories, opinions, and beliefs. Also, see information on framing issues on pp. 138-140.)

(1) The newsletter should adhere strictly to the purposes and principles of the organization. If you have made a commitment to focusing on one specific goal (such as protecting home schoolers' rights to educate their children without undue interference or regulation) and to maintaining unity among home schoolers in your state by not taking a position on approaches to education, beliefs, and principles, make sure the newsletter reflects this.

(2) You need to address several audiences at once. In the first place, the members are undoubtedly a diverse group with widely differing interests, commitments, political philosophies, religious beliefs, educational backgrounds, etc. You need to keep these differences in mind as you write, so the organization remains united and members are not upset. In addition, assume your newsletter will be read by legislators; think seriously before including disparaging remarks about the legislative process. Third, the media may read and quote from your newsletter. It is important to present a positive image of home schooling and appear to be reasonable and not outside of society. Finally, assume your adversaries will read your newsletter. Do not print inflammatory or unfounded statements about them. Do not help them by airing problems, conflicts, and divisions within your organization.

The need to address several audiences can seem frustrating and limiting at first. Communicating with such a diverse group is indeed a challenge. However, you may find that you get used to it and in fact it actually improves your newsletter; it certainly keeps you honest and on your toes!

(3) Do not print any advertising. Almost any ad will offend someone in your organization. Even if you find one which does not, you have set a precedent and will have a harder time refusing future requests for ads that will be divisive. Also, anytime you accept money from someone, he has some power over you.

Some practical suggestions you may find helpful:

(1) Make your newsletter schedule flexible, if possible. For example, publish four times a year with specific dates determined by the times at which newsletters are most needed that year, not by a set schedule. This allows you to select the most appropriate time to send out information.

(2) Colored paper is more expensive than white but makes the newsletter easily recognized and recovered from a stack of miscellaneous papers. Choose a light color for ease of reading and avoid colors that might have associations in your area

(3) Think seriously about the overall effect of the newsletter. Does it reflect the purpose and principles of your organization? Avoid a "slick" or glossy look even if you can get it inexpensively.

(4) Make the print as legible as possible. Include "white space" (blank space) so the newsletter looks attractive and inviting.

(5) Number and date each issue for easy identification.

(6) Include a table of contents.

(7) Printers' prices vary. Get several estimates. If possible, make your choice consistent with your organization's principles. Develop a strong working relationship with a reliable printer who can be a wonderful asset in times of crisis and stress.

(8) Using bulk mail is more work but can save lots of money.

(9) Keep a loose-leaf notebook of all back issues of your newsletter and encourage members to do the same.

(10) Reprint key articles from past newsletters and make them available to new members.

TELEPHONE TREES

Having a plan in which each member calls one or more other members to relay important information can be a great aid in a crisis when a simple message needs to be conveyed quickly. However, the written word (newsletters, emergency bulletins, post cards, etc.) is a much better and more effective way of communicating, especially if the message is at all complicated or something that members will need to refer to again as they discuss it with a legislator, etc. An informative newsletter also makes a telephone tree much more effective in a crisis, since members will already have background information and be prepared to deal with the information in the phone message.

ANNUAL CONFERENCES

An annual state-wide home schooling conference can serve many functions. It strengthens an organization by bringing its members together for a time of sharing and mutual support. It provides an excellent opportunity to communicate information to members and for members and leaders to meet together. It gives members a chance to gain new information and meet other home schoolers, including some from their local area. It is a welcome change for home schoolers to be in the majority. A conference can also provide much needed funds for the organization.

A few practical suggestions that might be helpful:

--Start small and keep it simple. This list is just ideas to stimulate your thinking; do not feel you need to do everything on the list. Enjoy the conference yourself!

--Begin with a site that is centrally located if at all possible. You can move to different parts of the state in succeeding years, although if you find a good site, it is much easier to keep using it.

Schools and universities are often less expensive than motels and other commercial sites. Visit the site, see the facilities, and find out what services are available (microphones, audio-visual equipment, coffee and juice, etc.). Find out what options are available for lunch. Are there restaurants near-by? Is there a place where people can eat brown bag lunches? What about parking?

--For a one day conference, 3 or 4 sessions that are each an hour to an hour and a half in length seem to work well. Offer a number of choices during each session. It is generally a good idea to offer a variety of sessions on different aspects of home schooling but avoid highly controversial or divisive topics. Try to present a balance of different perspectives and make it very clear in the description of the session what perspective is being presented. (For example, if a session on reading will stress the phonics method, say that; if a session on high school at home will emphasize alternatives to a purchased curriculum, make that clear.) Emphasize that speakers are presenting their own views, not necessarily those of the organization.

--Sessions on political strategy, working with the legislature and local school boards, etc., may not be as popular as those dealing with day-to-day concerns of home schooling parents, but it is important to offer them for people who are interested and to encourage others to become involved. Be sure to offer a session on any timely topics, such as pending legislation.

--Big name keynote speakers may increase attendance at a conference, but they also present a number of problems. Reliance on "experts" is counter to a grassroots organization's goal of empowering its members to solve their own problems. (For more information on this, see pp. 116-117.) Any speaker selected is likely to please one faction of home schoolers and disappoint others and therefore be divisive. Such speakers also tend to be expensive. Instead of keynote speeches, sessions presented by home schooling parents are generally well received, and strengthen the principles and purposes of a grassroots organization.

--Plan carefully for vendors of curriculum and related educational materials. It is important that various approaches to home schooling be welcomed and included. At the same time, presentations by vendors at a conference can compete with other speakers and promote specific approaches to education. This can threaten the unity of the conference and the organization's purpose and so should be carefully considered.

--You can publicize the conference through public service radio spots, posters in public buildings, etc., but it seems that the most effective publicity is your own newsletter, announcements in local support groups, and word of mouth among home schoolers.

--Preregistration by mail goes much more smoothly than registration on the day of the conference, unless you have a very small group. If possible, though, allow walk-in registrations for people who hear about the conference at the last minute.

--A written program makes it easier for people to find the location of their sessions and get other important information they need. An evaluation form gives people a chance to express their ideas and opinions and helps the planners of the next conference. Having people evaluate each session they attend gives some guidance in deciding which sessions and speakers to repeat.

--If you invite the media, consider designating a press or media room where information and a conference spokesperson will be rather than allowing the media full access to all sessions. This gives conference speakers and participants greater freedom for discussion and helps ensure that the media is not able to pick a highly unrepresentative or unflattering picture or sound "bite" for its representation of the event.

--An annual membership meeting can be held after the last session. This is a good time to discuss and vote on resolutions that cover positions the organization might adopt, such as opposition to legislation that would further regulate home schooling.

--Consider having a reception with simple refreshments after the conference for speakers and conference workers.

A STATE HANDBOOK

A handbook can be a multifaceted asset. It helps individual home schoolers plan, begin, and handle challenges and problems. It greatly strengthens the home schooling organization that produced it. Also, it serves as a tool to help people retain their freedoms and prevent issues from developing into legal and court fights. Among the topics that could be covered are: the importance of home schoolers' working together and ways this can be done; text and interpretation of laws, regulations, and policies directly related to home schooling; other laws that affect home schoolers; home schooling resources; working with the legislature to gain and maintain reasonable laws; dealing with public school officials; and winning support for home schooling. As an example, Wisconsin's handbook is available from Wisconsin Parents Association, P.O. Box 2502, Madison, WI 53701.

CONCLUSION

An inclusive, state-wide, united home schooling organization is a lot of work but well worth it. It is most likely to succeed and survive if it begins with a clear purpose that all home schoolers can support, such as to protect the right of parents to secure for their children an education consistent with their principles and beliefs. It can then welcome and unite all home schoolers. It takes careful and committed leadership and committed members to avoid divisions and distractions, to build slowly and carefully on a solid basis, and to stay focused on working through legislation and policy decisions rather than litigation. But a grassroots organization that empowers and relies on its members rather than outside experts is a strong, effective force in the fight to preserve and protect our rights and freedoms.

CHAPTER 15

COMMON QUESTIONS ABOUT HOME SCHOOLING

Home schoolers are frequently questioned by people who are sincerely interested in their approach to education as well as by critics who may be trying to discredit home schooling. It can be helpful to have thought through a series of questions and possible answers, beginning perhaps with those listed below and then adding your own information and other questions. This can be particularly valuable as you prepare to talk with a newspaper reporter or other representative of the media, to testify at a legislative hearing, or to meet with a public school official. Not only do you then have good points ready at your fingertips, but you can also approach the questioning more confidently and calmly, which helps you deal with unexpected questions.

Some of these questions are discussed in other chapters of this book. Rather than repeating the information, page references are given.

WHY ARE THRIVING HOME SCHOOLS NEEDED?

Home schools provide an important approach to education and an alternative to conventional schools. Because of their alternative nature, they also serve as proving grounds for new ideas about education and how children learn. The existence of

165

home schools and private schools ensures that the state does not have a monopoly in education and that families have a range of alternatives from which to choose the educational program that best suits their needs and abilities. Some children who have difficulty learning in a conventional school setting do very well learning at home. Home schools quickly lose their alternative quality when they are regulated by public schools, forced to submit to state-mandated standardized testing, or forced in other ways to become like conventional schools.

ARE LAWS THAT REGULATE HOME SCHOOLS NECESSARY?

No. See pp. 216-218, 226-228.

IF HOME SCHOOLING LAWS ARE UNAVOIDABLE, WHOSE RIGHTS NEED TO BE PROTECTED BY SUCH LAWS?

The rights of the state, of parents, and of children should be protected. See pp. 221-222.

SHOULD THE STATE REQUIRE THAT HOME SCHOOLERS TAKE STANDARDIZED TESTS?

Although home schooled children do well on standardized tests, state-mandated standardized testing is unwise for several reasons.

--Standardized tests can be a frighteningly effective means of control. If students are to score well, the curriculum needs to be geared to the tests. Thus state-mandated standardized tests would give the state too much control over private education. The state, rather than a child's parent, could decide when the child was ready for the tests, what tests would be used, how and where tests would be administered, and what would be done with the results.

166

--Standardized tests have numerous defects. They have been shown to be biased against women, minorities, creative thinkers, and anyone who does not have the values or experiences of the test makers. The tests do not measure what they claim to measure. They also overlook important qualities such as creativity, resourcefulness, good judgment, independence, and perseverance.

--Standardized tests reduce or eliminate the flexibility home schools need to function as alternatives to conventional schools.

--Standardized tests interfere with the learning process. By emphasizing and encouraging shallow, rote learning, they shift a student away from asking serious questions and learning through problem solving. Instead, tests encourage a student to focus on learning how to take tests. This reduces a child's interest in learning since answers are not as interesting or mentally rewarding as problems. In emphasizing "right" and "wrong" answers, tests imply a kind of certainty that does not exist or cannot be measured. The learning process is much more complex, non-linear, and dynamic than tests can measure. Test results are used to unfairly and inaccurately label children. Any test is basically a vote of "no confidence." And so on.

--A report issued by the National Commission on Testing Policy in May, 1990, recommended prohibiting standardized tests in elementary schools and strongly limiting their use by colleges and employers. This report is based on a three year study of scholarly reports on the subject.

--Even if a state requires standardized tests of its public school students, this is not an adequate reason for requiring them of private school students, including home schoolers. In keeping with recent studies such as one by the Carnegie Forum on Education and the Economy, some universities and states are now no longer administering or requiring such tests. For example, North Carolina has banned standardized testing for grades K-2 and similar bills have been introduced in other states.

SINCE REVIEW AND APPROVAL BY SCHOOL OFFICIALS SHOULD NOT BE TROUBLESOME TO CONSCIENTIOUS HOME SCHOOLERS, WHY NOT REQUIRE IT JUST TO BE SURE THAT HOME SCHOOLERS ARE GETTING A GOOD EDUCATION?

See pp. 233-234.

WHAT QUALIFICATIONS DOES A HOME SCHOOL TEACHER NEED?

To be an effective home school teacher, a parent should care about her child and be willing to spend time with him. This time and the opportunities that a home schooling parent has to observe her child mean that the parent can develop a clearer understanding of her child's interests, abilities, talents, and needs than a teacher who is responsible for many other students and who knows the child for only nine months. The parent's understanding puts her in a good position to help her child learn.

A home schooling parent should be interested in learning something himself and be willing to try different approaches to learning himself and to encourage his child to try different approaches. (Some things can be learned by reading a book, others by close observation, by using learning tools such as math manipulatives, by direct hands-on experience, by talking with others, etc.)

It is also helpful if a home schooling parent has problem solving abilities, a reasonable support system, and good judgment in knowing when and how to seek outside resources.

SHOULD STATE CERTIFICATION OF HOME SCHOOL TEACHERS BE REQUIRED?

No. See pp. 97, 237-238.

WHAT ABOUT THE FEW PARENTS WHO FAIL TO PROVIDE AN ADEQUATE EDUCATION?

There are very few such cases. Parents want what is best for their children. Home schooling is hard work requiring a substantial commitment of a parent's time and energy. Negligent parents are much more likely to use the free services of the local public schools. Also, given the stable and supportive environment of a home school and the opportunity for one-to-one contact with the "teacher," the vast majority of children learn a great deal, and parents do not need special training, expertise, or knowledge.

As is the case with any undertaking, a few people may fail to do a good job, especially since home schooling is a last resort for some children and families whom the schools and/or society have failed. This means there may be some problems. But an old legal maxim states, "Hard cases make bad law." In other words, a law designed to take care of the worst possible hypothetical case is almost certain to be long, difficult to enforce, and more likely to prevent good people from doing good than bad people from doing bad. It is unfair and accomplishes nothing to burden conscientious home schoolers with restrictions and regulations that do not solve the problem of high risk children but do damage the effectiveness of good home schools.

If a truant officer has reasonable evidence, she can prosecute the parents for truancy. If a home schooling family is suspected of child abuse, the problem can be handled as any other abuse case. Child abuse and home schooling are separate issues. No public, private, or home schooling law can protect a child from the tragedy of child abuse.

NOTE: Since home schooling is sometimes criticized as a "haven" for truants, home schoolers need to be prepared to discuss truancy issues such as these.

WHAT ARE THE MAJOR CAUSES OF TRUANCY?

• Stress from various sources • An educational system that tries to force parents and children to comply with mandates rather than offering them choices and incentives • Lack of alternative educational programs that would allow students to make maximum use of their widely varying talents, abilities, and learning styles • Labeling students as "learning disabled," "dyslexic," etc. and putting them into tracks that give them few if any choices, do not help them solve the real problems they may have, and seriously damage their confidence and self-esteem • Emphasizing rote learning, which is not particularly meaningful or exciting • Lack of involvement of parents and other caring adults in a child's education • Extending the compulsory school attendance law so that young people are required to stay in school longer. In some states, recent legislation requires school attendance until age 18 and offers few if any alternatives to a conventional classroom.

WHAT ARE SOME REASONABLE APPROACHES TO TRUANCY PROBLEMS?

--Approaches designed to offer truants constructive alternatives are more likely to be effective than those designed to punish the child and her parents. Providing incentives is more likely to work than relying on mandates.

--Providing alternative programs (such as home schooling or helping qualified high schoolers take courses in college or technical school) would help individual students find an approach to education that suits their interests, needs, and abilities.

--Granting a diploma to 16 year olds who pass a rigorous competency examination would allow qualified youth to move on to more appropriate activities such as college, employment, or volunteer service rather than forcing them to spend more time in conventional high school classrooms.

WHAT ABOUT SOCIALIZATION?

Many families find that home schooling offers more opportunities than conventional schooling for contact with a wide variety of people of differing backgrounds and ages. Home schooling families are involved in support groups and are also active in community organizations, their neighborhood, church, etc. Children interact with their peers through scouts, 4-H, interest groups, church groups, neighborhood activities, field trips, etc.

Some observers find that home schooled children become less peer dependent than children in conventional schools, which many parents and other adults see as an advantage. The interaction of 25 children in a classroom can have negative aspects such as intense competition and peer dependency. This leads many parents to feel that the social aspects of a classroom setting need not be duplicated and in fact may best be avoided. After all, school is the only place people are required to interact with a group of people who are all the same age.

Also see pp. 75, 78-80.

CAN HOME SCHOOLERS EARN HIGH SCHOOL DIPLOMAS AND GET INTO COLLEGE?

Yes. See pp. 74-75.

CHAPTER 16

FINDING ALLIES

Home schoolers need support from non-home schoolers. Although we strongly oppose labeling and categorizing people, for convenience we offer a few general categories here to help you think of ways you might approach different people. You will be more likely to gain their support if you emphasize points that will be of particular interest to each person.

--Private school people--Point out that once the state takes away the rights and liberties of one group, others will not be far behind. If home schools are subjected to increasing control by the public school hierarchy, will small private schools be next? When family values and individual liberties are at stake, is it not time to take a stand?

--Older people--Many remember one room schools; explain how well home schooling is working for you on a similar model. Ask how they feel about public schools' taking over family functions, such as providing preschool day care and resource centers that would supposedly teach parents how to parent.

--Minorities, perhaps especially Blacks--Point out that home schoolers are learning what labels such as "learning disabled," "at risk," "habitually truant" mean when they are used against you. Home schoolers want to work with other minority groups to fight against the trend toward state control of education and to support and encourage parental rights and choice in education. Also stress the need for choice and incentives in education rather than a standardized approach that mandates only one approach to learning.

--Small businesses--Explain the increasing costs of public schools and how high these costs will go if all the significant choices in education are eliminated. Businesses that believe in self-sufficiency and individual initiative might want to support home schoolers as one of the last groups of people who are working hard to maintain that spirit and tradition. Point out that our fight is really their fight as well.

--Farmers--Point out that property taxes will not go down unless there are challenges to the special interests that dominate public education. Home schoolers are one of the few groups committed to fighting against control of family life by the public school interests. Home schoolers need farmers' help; working with home schoolers is one way farmers can reduce the cost of education or at least prevent its increase.

--Civil libertarians, progressives, and true conservatives--Point out that individual worth, freedom, and independent expression are important values in a free society and that professional interest groups have become near monopolies more interested in their own interests than in those they are serving.

CHAPTER 17

WORKING WITH THE MEDIA

The vast majority of the general public sees home schooling through the eyes of the media, including radio, television, newspapers, and magazines. It is important for home schoolers to use the media to promote positive public opinion about home schooling. Positive articles in the press and appearances on radio and television can do a great deal to advance general acceptance of home schooling. This chapter presents ideas on understanding the media, preparing for and handling an interview, and dealing with representatives of the media.

PERSPECTIVES ON THE MEDIA

An understanding of the way the media functions and its expectations of home schoolers provides a valuable basis for dealing with representatives of the media. A few ideas:

--The media is not neutral on educational issues (or any other issues). It is not an independent and unbiased channel through which people get only pure facts. Everything that is reported is of necessity interpreted and presented from a certain perspective. With rare exceptions, both media representatives and their audience view education from the perspective of conventional education. Almost all reporters, readers, and viewers send their children to conventional schools and so have a vested interest in them. Reporters' normal contacts and sources of information are people who have a high stake in seeing conventional schools succeed and be viewed positively.

--The media is not accustomed to controversy about how education should be provided in a local community. The educational news reported in local and state papers deals primarily with school funding questions, school activities, athletics, special awards, etc.

--Editors, publishers, and producers are part of the economic infrastructure of conventional education, including everything from back-to-school ads to university rankings.

In discussing home schooling with media representatives, home schoolers should emphasize the diversity among home schoolers, including the variety of reasons they home school, the different ways they approach education, the range of religious and philosophical beliefs they hold, etc. Emphasizing the differences among home schoolers will help to prevent the media from stereotyping home schoolers and dismissing them as a weird group of fanatics. Home schoolers need support from as many non-home schoolers as possible, and broad support will be easier to get if the broad base of home schooling is accurately portrayed. Home schooling should not become a partisan issue or be linked to other issues. It is to our advantage as home schoolers to be seen as the underdogs that we really are.

The local press may well be the most advantageous place for articles about home schooling. A newspaper article about people from the community is more likely to impress the general public on a personal level than a more imposing article in the national press. An example of an excellent local newspaper story can be found on p. 266.

RESPONDING TO REQUESTS FROM THE MEDIA OR CONTACTING THE MEDIA YOURSELF

Contacts with media representatives provide opportunities for home schoolers to communicate with the general public. Seriously consider and discuss with other home schoolers any request from the media for an interview or radio or television appearance, even though talking with a reporter may at first seem overwhelming, perhaps because you have not had previous experience doing this. However, also be aware that media contacts carry the risk that inaccurate or misleading information could deliberately or inadvertently be conveyed.

Determine the reporter's objective. Most articles and/or programs about home schooling are human interest stories about families, or general background stories about home schooling as an educational alternative, or explorations of one or more controversial issues that seem to involve home schooling, or a combination of these. Controversial stories are often particularly attractive to the press but may be more challenging for you to handle smoothly. In such a case, you may prefer to respond to questions only in writing, so you have more time to consider your answers and less chance of being misunderstood and misquoted.

In some cases it may be best to refuse to be interviewed or participate in another way, for example, if the publication is very radical (either left or right), if the reporter is known to be very negative about home schooling, or if he has a reputation for quoting out of context or being difficult to deal with.

You can also initiate contact with the media. You could ask your local paper to run an article on home education in general and/or on your home schooling experience, for example. Or you may want to respond to an article or a radio or television program. Letters to the editor and calls you place during talk shows can also result in positive publicity. A state grassroots organization may issue press releases and announcements about meetings or conferences that you may want to use as a basis for contacting the media.

176

As in other areas of activity, however, do not act hastily on your own. Before making a move, particularly on an important issue, discuss your approach and strategy with other home schoolers. Without this kind of communication, you could easily make serious mistakes or work at cross purposes.

PREPARING FOR AN INTERVIEW

Consider the background, perspectives, etc. of the reporter and the media organization that she represents. Then select a home schooler from your area whose background, perspectives, and abilities would enable him to communicate effectively with the reporter. Decide whether to include children and how you will respond if the reporter asks to include children. (Many children benefit from practice before such an experience.)

If possible, find out what sorts of questions the reporter is planning to ask. It may be helpful to be prepared to answer questions such as: Why are you home schooling? Is it for religious reasons? Do you use a curriculum? Describe a typical day in your home school. What qualifies you to teach? Do you plan to teach your child at home when she is of high school age? How will your child be able to get a diploma or go to college? What about socialization? Peer group experiences important, are they not? Is your child going to be able to deal with the real world? What do your friends and relatives think of your home school? What does the law require of home schoolers? What is wrong with the state testing your children? If your child were to go to school, how would her grade placement be determined? What about the argument that the state has a responsibility to ensure that all children are receiving a good education? How are home schoolers held accountable? What about home schoolers who abuse the law? What about child abuse among home schoolers? What is so bad about the public schools? May I ask your child some questions? Other common questions about home schooling are in Chapter 15.

Gather background information. Review your own experiences and talk with other home schoolers. Read a variety of articles and books on home schooling and prepare to share some quotes with the reporter. If you quote others, the reporter cannot argue with you personally on that particular point.

Give the reporter articles from the local, state, and national press on home schooling and background information from home schooling authors, newsletters, magazines, and publishers. Read over any material to be sure it does not make points that will work against home schoolers. Think through how the material is likely to be used by the reporter.

DURING THE INTERVIEW

Relax. As a home schooler you have reason to feel confident of your position. Try to be brief in your answers and make the most important points before going into detail. Remember that your comments will probably be condensed before they are printed or broadcast. Be polite and courteous, no matter how heated the discussion. Rudeness does not win friends, however just the cause.

Speak only for yourself or the group you are specifically authorized to represent. (Being a member of an organization does not authorize you to speak for that organization.) Avoid making sweeping statements or speaking for all home schoolers. But at the same time, try to convey that home schoolers are a diverse group with a wide variety of reasons for home schooling.

Match your presentation to your audience. Think in terms of most people's ideas about conventional education and try to translate your ideas and experiences into terms most people can understand. Keep your answers as basic and simple as possible; you will be less likely to be misunderstood or misquoted.

Avoid negative comments about public schools, legislators, school boards, superintendents, etc. Remember that reporters are often interested in advancing controversy, but such conflicts rarely help one's own cause or public image; instead they often hurt both.

Do not jeopardize relations with allies or potential allies by speaking for them or repeating a position that might be embarrassing for them, forcing them to deny what you said, or making them distrustful of you and other home schoolers.

Do not rely on or over-emphasize constitutional rights, which are very important but also complex and seldom accurately presented in the media. It may be better for home schoolers to emphasize that we are a small minority of the total population, that we act responsibly, that our children do well academically and socially.

Remember that you can refuse to answer a question and change the subject. You can also repeat an answer you have already given if you do not want to say more on a topic or be drawn into controversy.

FOLLOW-UP

Remember that few (in any) articles or news reports are perfect; so if the article or report is basically accurate or positive, thank the reporter. Remain in contact with him, sending articles you think may be of interest, keeping him posted on further developments, etc. A reasonable reporter who is willing to listen can be a very valuable ally.

If the article is inaccurate, unfair, or negative, write a letter to the editor and ask others to do the same. State your objections and counter-arguments clearly, but be polite. If possible, continue to send the reporter information about home schooling.

CHAPTER 18

RESEARCH ON HOME SCHOOLING

Interest in doing research on home schoolers is growing. Increasingly home schoolers are being asked to fill out questionnaires and participate in research studies. Our first response may be to feel flattered. After all, we know we are doing a good job and have interesting stories to tell. It is about time other people caught on and wanted to know more about us. This will give us a chance to share some of what we have learned. We are confident that research results would reveal and "prove" the strengths of home schooling and home schoolers. And maybe research would help convince our adversaries that home schooling is an acceptable alternative and does not need state regulation. It would certainly be a useful tool to have available in court cases, legislative battles, and any time we need to document the strength of home schooling. On a personal level, some of us would like to fill out a questionnaire, just to see how well we can answer the questions and "measure up."

However, before we wholeheartedly embrace research and agree to participate in studies, we need to take a much closer look at what is involved. We need to ask what effect such research will have on the home schooling movement, whether such educational research is really as scientific and accurate as it claims to be, who will benefit from such research, whether such research is necessary, what alternatives exist for gathering additional information about home schoolers, and how home schoolers can respond to research requests.

180

WHAT EFFECT WOULD EDUCATIONAL RESEARCH HAVE ON THE HOME SCHOOLING MOVEMENT?

(1) Research on home schooling strongly promotes the values and practices of conventional schooling, an effect which is very serious, especially since many of us are home schooling precisely because we object strongly to these values and practices. Among the ways research promotes these values are:

--Conventional school values and practices dominate the background, training, and experience of educational researchers. They are accustomed to using data sets, research methods, and questions that are suited to conventional schools, so they inevitably attempt to fit home schoolers into these categories. They ask, in effect, "How well do home schoolers do what conventional schools do?" rather than asking, "What do home schoolers do that is of value?" This generally applies even if a researcher has had personal experience with home schooling, partly because participation in the conventional educational system is a prerequisite to getting credentials for doing research that is recognized and accepted in most educational settings and journals. Evidence of researchers' bias is readily found in the language used, the types of questions asked, and the assumptions underlying home schooling research questionnaires.

--A home schooler filling out a questionnaire gets the clear message that she should be following conventional school values and practices. A question like, "How many hours a week do you teach reading?" clearly implies that she had better be teaching reading, and for quite a few hours a week at that. Once more the message is sent to home schoolers, "You had better make sure you are conforming with what is expected of conventional schools." Again home schools are pushed in the direction of becoming like conventional schools and away from the advantages they offer as alternatives to conventional schools.

--Research studies compare home schoolers with conventional schoolers. The studies are clearly implying that the standard which should be held up for home schoolers, against which they should be measured, is that of conventional schools. This does not give any credit to home schoolers whose goals and values are different from those of conventional schools.

(2) Research studies weaken a grassroots movement in several ways, including these:

--Participating in research gives credence and importance to quantitative studies rather than to winning support for home schooling by having home schoolers tell their own stories and share their experiences through presentations to groups in their communities, newspaper stories, etc. It is another example of relying on "experts" instead of empowering themselves.

--Studies can divide home schoolers by emphasizing differences among them as shown in their responses to questions and to research surveys in general.

--As a general strategy, it is better for a small minority like home schoolers to keep the opposition guessing than to reveal too much about themselves.

(3) Research could provide data and arguments that opponents of home schooling could use to support their demands for greater regulation of home schooling. For example, if a study reveals that some, or many, or most home schoolers voluntarily do something, such as use a purchased curriculum, or administer standardized tests, or keep detailed records, opponents of home schooling could argue that these are generally acceptable to home schoolers and should be required of them. In other words, the research could be used to force these practices on home schoolers, especially if a large majority of them already seem to fit conventional school expectations.

In addition, and perhaps even more serious, once the role that research findings should play in determining home school regulation is accepted, there is no end to the regulation that can and will be required, based on research. For example, home schoolers have been reported to score as well as or better than their conventional school counterparts on standardized tests. Additional research is now showing that these tests are questionable at best and that other means of assessment (such as portfolio assessment) are needed in addition to, if not in place of, such tests. Do home schoolers want to be subjected to this additional requirement or any others? (Research studies have been used to justify and support virtually all the practices of conventional schools.)

(4) The right of a family to home school has a solid foundation. In agreeing to be the subject of research, home schoolers are implicitly agreeing that we need to be judged and assessed. We are thereby surrendering an important fundamental right. If we get into this game of proving what we can do by conventional standards, we are giving up one of our most important rights.

(5) Because research studies emphasize conventional school values and practices, they move home schoolers away from the cutting edge of educational alternatives and innovations and limit the contribution we could make to the understanding of how children learn and how adults can assist them.

(6) On an emotional level, when measured against what really matters, research is found wanting and can be harmful. It distorts and damages our self-image, our self-esteem, and our confidence. Among other things:

--Research quantifies and thus dehumanizes people. Instead of wonderful, alive, unique individuals, our children become black marks on a score sheet; our families become numbers, part of a set.

--Research is an invasion of privacy, even if anonymity is guaranteed. We have still been asked questions we might have preferred not to answer; we have still been singled out for scrutiny.

--The emotional impact of filling out a survey can be much like that of taking a standardized test. The implication is that someone, somewhere knows what we should be doing; that there are right answers, or at least better answers. The questions almost seem to say, "You should be teaching this many hours a week, you should be going on field trips, you should be participating in a support group, etc." This encourages people to figure out what they should be doing so they can report it on a survey, and they may lose sight of the effect such an action will have on their children. Research seems to render a judgment on home schoolers; it does not encourage them to become empowered and make their own decisions.

--Research promotes conventional school values and practices (see above). This may undermine the confidence of some home schoolers who are trying to find alternatives to conventional schooling that will better serve the needs of their families.

--Questionnaires usually begin with a "guilt trip" about how important the study is and how much home schoolers' help is needed. The many home schoolers who want to do whatever they can to support the home schooling cause may be particularly vulnerable to pleas of this type and need to realize that research has serious potential problems.

ARE RESEARCH RESULTS ACCURATE?

The history of social science research, including educational research, is filled with problems, criticisms, accusations, and doubts. Space does not permit a thorough discussion, but among the most important points that pertain to home schooling research are:

--Most topics included in the social sciences cannot be studied scientifically. Home schooling cannot be quantified or measured. For example, there is no common agreement about what it means to be educated or how a researcher determines when someone is educated. To try to make their studies more "scientific," researchers sometimes choose instead variables that seem easier to measure, like how many hours a day a child spends reading. (Even this is complicated. For example, if in an hour, one child quickly skims a book and remembers little, a second child reads uncritically and recalls many details, and a third child covers only a few pages but thinks a lot about the subject, are all three "reading?") If a researcher studies only things that can easily be measured, like how many years the subject of research has been home schooling or the subject's age, the results are simply a collection of statistics and do not reveal much.

--Responses people give are influenced both by what the researcher asks and how she asks it. Definitions of terms are also a problem. If a researcher asks whether a home schooler is "home schooling for political reasons," what does the researcher think she is asking, what does the home schooler mean by his answer, and how does a person reading the research results interpret the question and the answer? Sometimes researchers try to correct this problem by simply reporting that a certain number or per cent of home schoolers said they were home schooling for political reasons. But if it is not clear what this means, what is the point of doing the research?

--Subjects' realization that they are being observed changes their behavior. Some give answers intended to please the researcher rather than those which would be accurate or give more complete information. Others hide information or distort things. Others refuse to participate. (Researchers account for those who refuse by having what they consider enough other respondents with similar characteristics [income, education, religious background, age, sex, place of residence, etc.]. But one never knows what the non-respondents really represent, which limits the accuracy of researchers' conclusions, especially when dealing with a small minority.)

--Research data by definition must be interpreted; and a researcher's experiences, beliefs, and biases influence his interpretations. This adds more uncertainty and ambiguity to the research.

--The most important parts of home schooling (the look of joy on a child's face as she discovers something, the recovered self-esteem of a child who had been labeled "learning disabled" by a conventional school) cannot be captured and recorded in quantitative or "scientific" studies. Therefore research gives a misleading picture of home schooling when it claims to show the strengths of home schooling but fails to study or report the most important ones.

--Despite these and other limitations, complications, and ambiguities, researchers present their results as facts, using numbers, graphs, charts, and similar devises to give the illusion of scientific accuracy. This is at best misleading and occasionally downright dishonest.

WHO BENEFITS FROM HOME SCHOOLING RESEARCH?

Given all these problems and pitfalls, why would anyone do research on home schooling? Who benefits? Obviously, researchers and the universities and other institutions with which they work or who support and use their work benefit directly in terms of money received and increased status and prestige. Home schooling research may be particularly in vogue now, making it easier to get grants and other support for home schooling research than for other seemingly less timely topics. But when there are more than 100,000 articles published each year (as reported in *Phi Delta Kappan*, Vol. 71, No. 3, Nov., 1989, p. 226), there must be intense pressure on graduate students, instructors, and professors alike to find an original topic. Do home schoolers have an obligation to serve as fodder for this arm of the educational establishment?

IS HOME SCHOOLING RESEARCH NECESSARY?

No. Parents have the right to home school their children, and there is no substantial evidence that home schoolers are a problem. Note, for example, that essentially all the published stories about home schoolers are positive. (How many cover stories have appeared: "Home Schooling: The New Menace to Our Young?")

In addition, research is not effective. No matter how positive the results, research will not stop or significantly diminish opposition to home schooling. People who are already open-minded about the home school or tending to support it may say, "Oh, okay, since the studies show home schoolers do so well by conventional school standards, I'll support you." But people tend to hear what they want to hear, and positive research results are highly unlikely to change home schooling policies. Determined opponents of home schooling will argue, "The report shows that all the home schoolers who responded to the survey are doing a good job. But what inadequate home schooler would fill out such a survey honestly? Anyway, we still need regulation to prevent someone from doing a bad job in the future."

Given the potential problems outlined above, and the fact that there are better ways (see next question) of gathering information about home schooling, if such information is really needed, does it make sense for home schoolers to risk participating in studies which are unnecessary and ineffective?

ALTERNATIVES TO RESEARCH

There may be times when it is handy to cite research studies. In addition, some allies and potential supporters of home schooling claim that more needs to be known about home schooling. (We the authors do not agree, but nevertheless, that is how some people feel.) Is there an alternative to research, any other way to gather information that could be used to gain support for home schooling?

Case studies could be used. Home schoolers who are willing to share their experiences could do so, and these could be presented as just what they are--first person accounts of a particular experience. Few generalizations could be drawn from these reports, but as was shown above, accurate generalizations cannot be drawn from research data either. At least with case studies one would have a view of what home schooling is like for a few families. And some of the stories home schoolers have to tell are outstanding. Case studies are limited, too, but they are more honest about their limitations, and at least they come closer to conveying the uniqueness and value of an individual human life than a research study can.

Home schoolers like to talk about the exciting experiences they have had, discoveries they have made, things they have accomplished. Some feel they should participate in research so they can tell their story and help other home schoolers or potential home schoolers. This is an understandable and commendable reaction. However, for reasons given above, these people would probably contribute more to the cause of home schooling and have a more satisfying experience if they were willing to speak to groups about home schooling, testify at legislative hearings, be featured in a local newspaper story, write an article about their experiences, etc.

Rational, logical, legal, constitutional, moral, and practical arguments can be given to support home schooling. (See pp. 219-240 for examples.) It is much better for home schoolers to provide such arguments, plus case studies, than to give in to researchers' demands and participate in studies to show that home schooling is acceptable.

188

RESPONDING TO RESEARCH REQUESTS

A home schooler who receives a request for information for a research study has several options. If her honest response is to want to throw it in the trash, unread, she can do that and rest assured that she has not damaged the home schooling movement's chances for success--in fact, she may have made a positive contribution. Or she can read it and decide what to do on the basis of an honest assessment of her reaction. If she agrees with the values and approach of the researcher and wants to support them even at the risk of dividing or weakening the home schooling movement, she can send in the questionnaire. If her response is to feel that the questionnaire is objectionable and an invasion of privacy (even if she has been assured anonymity), she can refuse to fill it out. Or she can refuse to respond to the questions but send the researcher a letter explaining her objections, concerns, and reasons for refusing.

It can be argued that if home schoolers who refuse to adopt conventional school values refuse to respond to research requests, research data will be weighted even more heavily in favor of more conventional home schoolers and therefore be even more misleading. This is logically accurate. However, the problems and distortions of social science research would not be corrected even if every home schooler participated in a given study. Does it make sense to participate in a misleading and potentially harmful research study just so it will be a little bit less misleading and harmful?

CHAPTER 19

WORKING ON THE NATIONAL LEVEL

Although many home schoolers as individuals or as members of non-home schooling interest groups are active in various aspects of federal legislation, there is little need or reason for home schoolers as a group to become politically active on the federal level.

There is little likelihood of federal legislation to regulate home schooling. Educational policy in this country is decided on the state and local level. The federal government's role in education is limited to funding programs for special needs, supporting research, and providing financial aid for students in higher education. This limitation is appropriate since federal efforts tend to result in greater uniformity and larger, more distant bureaucracies. Of course home schoolers should remain alert and not assume that no federal home schooling law will ever be introduced, but it seems unlikely and there would undoubtedly be warning signs.

If federal legislation were to be introduced which does not directly regulate home schooling but seems so closely related to home schooling that home schoolers as a group should consider becoming involved, home schoolers need a clear basis for deciding whether to get involved and what strategy to follow. Home schoolers should pick their battles carefully, considering factors such as: • What precisely is at issue? • How directly does it affect us as home schoolers? • What arguments can be made for the proposal? What arguments against it? • Who else is impacted? • Who would our allies be? Who would be against us? • What forces are working to influence the legislature and other public officials involved? • Do we have the resources to handle this issue effectively? • Would this involvement be a sensible use of our resources?

In developing strategy, the following questions also need to be answered: • Specifically what does the bill provide and what will it do? • Who proposed it and why? • Who supports it and why? • Who opposes it and why? • What is wrong with it? • Who needs to be persuaded to vote our way? • What arguments are best? • Who should make the arguments? • When should this be done?

It would be unwise for home schoolers to try to introduce federal legislation to protect home schooling. Legislation can unfairly restrict home schooling, but it cannot protect home schoolers from being drawn into the demands and requirements of the educational establishment. We must remain alert and fight the continual efforts of the educational establishment to make us like them. We need to learn a lesson from large private schools. No legislation was ever passed requiring them to become like the public schools, and yet the vast majority of them are. Home schoolers are better off with a variety of state laws and the option of working on the state level to change a law or moving to a state with a better law. Even if a law or constitutional amendment could be devised that would really protect home schoolers, the work to gain support for it would need to be done first on the local and state level.

It would be very unwise for the home schooling movement to become involved in any other issues on a national level. Such mixing of causes would inevitably divide the movement, since there are no other issues on which all home schoolers can agree. Home schoolers need to remain united and nonpartisan in order to have the best chance of regaining and maintaining reasonable home schooling laws. Home schoolers who want to become involved in other national issues can certainly do that as individuals and as members of other organizations which are focused on those issues.

Finally, home schoolers should not allow themselves to be drawn as home schoolers into a personal or political agenda which is larger than home schooling. Such efforts may use home schoolers and end up hurting them politically at the national and state and local levels.

What would make sense is for home schoolers from different states to exchange information about experiences they have had with legislation, litigation, and regulation in their states. This could occur at a national conference, through a written newsletter, etc. but should not be carried out through a centralized, top-down organization relying on experts, because that undermines grassroots organizations. Any such national effort should include all interested home schoolers as equal participants regardless of their approach to education or their religious or philosophical beliefs. In this way grassroots organizations in different states could support each other, network, share resources, and strengthen one another so each would be better prepared to make decisions and handle the challenges it faces in its own unique situation in its own state.

PART V

COUNTERING RESTRICTIVE LAWS

CHAPTER 20

READING AND INTERPRETING LAWS YOURSELF

Important note: Nothing in this book is intended or should be taken as the giving of legal advice. This book is not intended to substitute for privately retained legal counsel.

Home schoolers need to work with laws in order to protect their rights and to make the best of the laws and regulations in their states. Some home schoolers begin by investigating the role laws play in our society and then obtaining a copy of laws relating to home schools and reading and interpreting them for themselves. This chapter suggests ways to do this and also presents ideas to consider if an attorney is needed.

PERSPECTIVES ON LAWS

Law should be kept in perspective. It is just one of the ways a society expresses its principles and beliefs and indicates what it will and will not accept. Law is only one means of maintaining social order. Most people decide to act in a certain way because they think or believe the action is right. They avoid other actions because they think or believe those actions are wrong, not because the actions are illegal. This is the only way in which a society can continue to function. For example, most people believe it is wrong to take someone else's possessions, so they do not steal. Theft is illegal and thieves are sometimes punished, but these facts are not what prevents most people from stealing. If this were not the case, a society could not pass enough laws and hire enough police, prosecutors, judges, and jailers to protect private property. Most social order exists because the citizens of a society agree on what is acceptable behavior. Laws are needed when members of a society cannot agree. This means that if everyone could agree that parents have a right to educate their own children and can be trusted to do this, home schooling laws and regulations would be unnecessary. However, until home schooling is once again accepted in this way, home schoolers will have to deal with home schooling laws.

Valuable perspective also comes from viewing the law as a process, rather than a finished product. A law sets a direction, but it does not make a once-and-for-all final decision. It is not set in stone. In a very real sense, a law is only worth the value of the paper it is printed on, because the way a society interprets and enforces a law determines its real meaning and value. Having a law on the books does not have any effect unless someone enforces it or exercises the rights it grants. Some laws are meaningless because they are not enforced. On the other hand, sometimes a law is passed which is unconstitutional or violates a basic right, but if no one objects, this law can be enforced and become accepted practice. It is part of our responsibility as citizens to ensure that laws are fair and protect basic rights. Law can be a great ally and protector, but it is also just a tool which cannot do anything for us unless we use it. It is also part of our responsibility as citizens to participate in the writing and revising of laws.

If, despite our best efforts, a law is passed which is unconstitutional or morally wrong or violates basic rights, we have to decide whether we will obey that law or refuse to obey it and handle the consequences. We abandon our responsibilities when we decide to do something simply because it is required by law without determining whether that law is a just law. We should think seriously therefore before we say, "I know this practice is wrong, but it is what the law requires, so I will do it." There may sometimes be good reasons for obeying an unjust law, but we should be clear about what those reasons are.

Similarly we need to decide whether we will comply with policies, regulations, and Attorney General's opinions. They may carry significant weight, but they do not have the same force as statutes and in certain instances are no more than opinions. It is incumbent upon us that we seriously consider whether we should comply and what our compliance will cost us, our children, other home schoolers, and the general public. From a practical standpoint we cannot simply ignore these policies and regulations, because often they are supported by the authority of the office of the person who formulated them and validated by practice. But we should remember that they are based on interpretations of the law and that they can be changed without changing the law. Practically speaking this means that we can negotiate a change in a policy without having to go through the whole process of having a new law passed.

THE IMPORTANCE OF READING LAWS

Home schoolers (and other citizens) should read the actual text of laws themselves for at least four reasons. First, knowledge of the law is important so we know what we are to obey and what the consequences may be if we do not. Often the best way to understand what the law says is to read it ourselves. Once we know what a law says word for word, we can present ourselves, and if necessary defend ourselves, with greater confidence. If we are in a conflict, this confidence makes a big difference in how we act and how our adversary views us and reacts.

Second, we may be in a better position to recognize the relevant portions of a law than anyone we could hire or ask to do it for us. Self-interest is an excellent motivator. Our future will be influenced by interpretations of home schooling laws, so we have strong incentive to study the law carefully. It often takes a lot of time and careful attention to detail to interpret a law or prepare a court case. The person most directly involved may be the most willing and strongly motivated to do this exacting work. Also, doing at least part of our own research may be the only affordable option, given the cost of lawyers' time. To be sure, experience helps, and legal training can be an asset. But in reading and interpreting home schooling laws, for example, our experience with home schooling may be as valuable as (or even more valuable than) the experience of a lawyer who has read many laws that have nothing to do with home schooling and few if any that relate to home schooling. (If you are considering contacting an attorney, see "Working with an Attorney" below.)

A third reason to read the law is that if we do not know what our rights are, we cannot be sure we are getting the protection to which we are entitled. We are literally "at the mercy of the court." For example, most states have a law that requires a child to have certain immunizations before entering school. Such laws often provide that a parent can waive this requirement by signing a statement that she objects to immunization for personal, medical, or religious reasons. However, schools may not notify parents of this right. In effect, if a parent is not familiar with the law, that right does not exist for her. The phrase "exercise one's rights" is telling. Like muscles, rights must be exercised or they weaken. And before we can exercise our rights, we have to know what they are.

As we gain experience reading the law, a fourth reason becomes clear. Few laws are so straight-forward that there is no question as to their intent or application. Most laws need to be interpreted before they can be obeyed or enforced. Our familiarity with issues, details, and nuances increases our ability to apply a law to our particular circumstances. To be sure that the interpretation given to a law will be most beneficial to us, we must interpret it ourselves, which means we must read it ourselves.

In short, in a government based on law, the citizens are the custodians of the law. If we simply accept legal experts' interpretation of the law or if we allow school officials to enforce their interpretation of the law (which quite likely will be different from ours), we will lose our rights and responsibilities in the law. We must read and interpret the law ourselves.

HOW TO READ LAWS

How then does one get started reading laws? First, accept the fact that laws are not written so they will be as accessible as possible to ordinary citizens. However, although not in the language most people use in dinner conversation, they are in English. If you have not read your state's laws relating to home schooling, this would be a good place to start. (See p. 12 for suggestions for ways of obtaining these laws.) Reading proposed legislation is also a good idea; then you can share your views with your legislators. Copies of bills being considered by the legislature can be obtained from your legislator or in many states by calling a legislative service agency, sometimes through an 800 telephone number.

Space does not allow a discussion of how to do more extensive legal research, but it is based on a logical system and is not too difficult. You certainly do not have to be a trained lawyer. While you are reading laws, it is also a good idea to read court cases that have interpreted and thus shaped these laws.

Two helpful books on locating and reading laws are *Using a Law Library*, published by HALT, Inc. and Stephen Elias's *Legal Research*. Two books that have excellent information on home schooling laws and their foundations are John Holt's *Teach Your Own*, pp. 271-324, and John W. Whitehead and Wendell R. Bird's *Home Education and Constitutional Liberties*.

HOW TO INTERPRET LAWS

Be sure to formulate your own interpretation of laws that concern you. Do not let someone else (especially a person with different goals, priorities, and perspectives, such as a public school official) interpret laws for you. It is a good idea to discuss interpretations of laws with other home schoolers, but do not neglect to interpret them yourself just because someone you trust has already done so. You may discover a new insight or interpretation that can be very valuable. As you interpret laws, use common sense, look at words with fresh eyes, and do not hesitate to try to interpret them in a way that will be to your advantage. This is a time when reasonable self-interest is appropriate.

Wisconsin's home schooling law provides an example of how laws can be interpreted using common sense. The law requires that a home school "provide at least 875 hours of instruction each school year." No definition of "instruction" is given. In planning and recording these hours, many parents consider the variety of ways in which instruction can take place. In addition to the conventional "teacher talks and student listens," students can be instructed by books (which they read themselves and/or a parent studies with them); by workbooks and exercise sheets; by hands-on experiments and close observations which give them a chance to discover things for themselves; by educational audio-visual materials (films, records, VCR tapes, audio tapes, etc.); by hands-on experiences such as field trips, "practical" studies (home economics, vocational education, typing, etc.); by educational games; and by other methods. This reasonable interpretation is supported by the fact that students in public schools are "instructed" in these ways. Home schoolers in Wisconsin interpreted the law themselves and acted on it. They did not ask the Department of Public Instruction or local public school officials what the law meant by "instruction."

Look with fresh eyes at the constitution of your state, and do not let yourself be limited by the statutes, regulations, procedures, and policies regarding education that have grown up based on common agreement rather than the constitution. For example, some state constitutions grant the state superintendent of education authority over public education, but not private. If this is the case in your state, you can argue that your state department of education does not have authority over home schools, which are private.

Another key to interpreting laws is legislative intent. You can argue that a law should be interpreted in a certain way because that was the intent of the legislature that passed it. If you are involved in the passage of a home schooling law, pay careful attention to the legislature's intent as revealed in the original version of the legislation, amendments, statements by legislators in response to testimony, and the way legislators vote. If the home schooling law was enacted before you became interested in it, try to find out about legislative intent by talking with home schoolers who were involved in its passage and with legislators who supported it.

One important word of caution--do not use your confidence in working with the law to jump into a lawsuit or a court case. Litigation is complex, expensive, and difficult to control. For more information, see pp. 144-147.

WORKING WITH AN ATTORNEY

Note: Rather than hiring an attorney, some home schoolers who want additional information and support for a meeting with a school official or other potentially difficult situation, ask another home schooler, possibly one who has had experience with a similar situation, to help them prepare and to accompany them to the meeting.

If you decide you need an attorney, the following suggestions may be helpful:

--The attorney needs to accept and be willing to work for your principles, beliefs, and practices. For example, if your major concerns are protecting parents' and children's rights and preserving the integrity of the family, make sure your attorney will work with you for this. Your attorney must accept and be prepared to defend the approach to home schooling you have chosen.

--The attorney needs to understand your local community. Judges consider community practice in making their decisions, and the climate of opinion within a community can influence the outcome of a case. This is one reason why local attorneys often are a better resource than "outside experts." Also, an attorney from your community is often better respected and not viewed with the suspicion attorneys from outside the community may engender.

--Make sure the attorney will listen to you, accept your input, and let you make decisions. You are looking for an attorney who will work with you, not an expert who will simply take over the whole case and run it for you. Your involvement is crucial because you are the one who is most directly involved in the case, who knows what direction you want to go, and who will have to live with the outcome.

--It is not essential that you find an attorney who has been personally involved in home schooling or who has had experience with home schooling cases. Your ideas and understanding of the law can be a tremendous help. Consider giving your attorney a copy of this book. Point out the sections that are particularly important to you and with which you agree.

--It is particularly important to discuss your approach with your attorney if he has experience, either personally or professionally or both, with home schooling. Home schoolers have many different approaches to beliefs, philosophy of education, educational methods, etc. It may be a real problem to try to work with an attorney whose approach to home schooling is different from yours. For example, an attorney who feels that every home school should use a purchased curriculum might find it difficult to represent a family whose home school is based on a learner-led approach to learning. As another example, there may be home schoolers who feel state-mandated standardized testing is an acceptable requirement, while others feel it is an unnecessary and harmful intrusion. It would not work well to have an attorney who accepted state-mandated standardized testing trying to defend a home schooler who was fighting this kind of state interference.

CHAPTER 21

WORKING WITH THE LEGISLATURE

This chapter provides information on the legislative process and suggestions for ways to contact your state legislators, either to establish a working relationship before there is a crisis or to gain their support after home schooling legislation has been introduced. Suggestions for testifying at a legislative hearing are also given.

HOW A BILL BECOMES A LAW

Note: The following steps are typical. Precise rules and specifics of who does what will vary from state to state.

1. When a legislator has an idea for a new law or a change in an existing law, he has it drafted as a bill. Typically either a legislative service agency composed of attorneys or the staff of a legislative committee will draft it.

2. One or more legislators introduce the bill by having the Chief Clerk of the Assembly/House or Senate or both record it and assign it a number. At this point the bill may become available to the general public for the first time; before this it can be kept secret in some states.

3. Although a hearing is not required, one is held on most bills. The chairperson of the appropriate committee schedules the hearing, so she has considerable power in deciding whether a bill gets a hearing and how quickly and whether the full committee votes on it. Hearings are open to the public, and anyone may speak and/or register for or against the bill. The committee usually goes into executive session to amend and vote on the bill. This may happen on the same day as the hearing or later; if the bill is controversial or the hearing draws a large number of people, the chairperson will often delay the executive session. Amendments to the bill made by legislators during executive session or later can result in a much different bill from the one considered at the public hearing.

4. The bill is scheduled for floor debate by the full house or senate. This is often done by a committee responsible for legislative rules. A bill can die in this committee if it is not scheduled. Toward the end of a legislative session, this can happen fairly often.

5. The bil! is debated and voted on by either the full Assembly/House or Senate and passed or defeated, with or without amendments.

6. If passed by one house, the bill goes to the other house of the legislature and steps three, four, and five are repeated. If the bill is amended further in the second house, these amendments must be passed by the first house before the bill goes to the governor for signature. (Sometimes a conference committee composed of representatives from both legislative bodies will work to reach agreement on differences between the two versions of the bill.)

7. The bill becomes law when signed by the governor. If the governor vetoes the bill, both houses of the legislature must override the veto, usually by a two-thirds majority, for the bill to become law.

CONTACTING YOUR LEGISLATORS

INITIAL CONTACT WITH YOUR LEGISLATORS

Your state representative and senator can be a big asset in a number of situations, including when the legislature is considering a home schooling bill and sometimes when you are contacted by public school officials and/or social service workers. It is helpful to contact your legislators before such situations arise. Their names, addresses, and phone numbers are available at local libraries or in some states through a legislative 800 number. Ways of contacting your legislators include:

--A letter of introduction can be written (see samples).

--Many legislators have open meetings with their constituents. Call the office in your district to find out when and where such meetings are held.

--You can make an appointment to meet with her at the office.

--You can invite him to speak to your support group. Groups that include more than one district sometimes invite a senator and several representatives.

--An effective way to gain a legislator's support for home schooling is having her visit you in your home before there is a crisis. You can share some of what you are doing in your home school and your positive feelings about it.

Whatever approach you take, legislators will be more likely to support home schooling if they have had positive encounters with home schoolers as real people, not just as statistics. A particularly good time to get to know a legislator is while he is a candidate for election or re-election. But if there will not be an election within the next few months, do not wait for one.

(Continued on p. 210.)

SAMPLE LETTER OF INTRODUCTION TO A
LEGISLATOR--VERSION 1

Your street address
City, state, zip
Date

The Honorable (full name)
Member of Assembly/House or Senate
State Capitol Building
City, state, zip

Sir (or Madam):

This letter is to introduce our family to you and to share with you our interest in home education.

In 19__, the (name of your state) Legislature enacted our current home schooling law, statute 000 entitled _____, which allows parents to meet the requirement of the compulsory school attendance law by conducting a home school. We have been conducting such a program since (date), and are very pleased with the results. We are grateful that the legislature made such an important educational alternative available to the citizens of (name of state).

If the home schooling law is reasonable, you could add something like:

The law has worked well since it was enacted. It holds home schoolers accountable and ensures that the compulsory school attendance law can be applied to home schoolers. There is no evidence that any further regulation of home schoolers is necessary; in fact, increased regulation could be detrimental.

Or, if the home schooling law is unreasonable, you might say something like:

The law has not worked well since it was enacted. It has major problems and results in unfair treatment of home schoolers. There is strong evidence that this law should be changed because ...

If you would like any further information about home schooling in general or about our family's experience, let us know.

Sincerely yours,

Your signature

Your full name

SAMPLE LETTER 0F INTRODUCTION TO A LEGISLATOR--VERSION 2

Your street address
City, state, zip
Date

The Honorable (full name)
Member of Assembly/House or Senate
State Capitol Building
City, state, and zip

Sir (or Madam):

I am writing as a constituent to share with you our family's very positive experience (or our family's somewhat negative experience) as a result of the Legislature's passage of the current home schooling law (statute 000 [fill in name of law]). It allows parents to meet the requirements of the compulsory school attendance law by conducting a home school.

We have been home schooling since (date) and are very pleased with the results. John's reading is greatly improved, and

208

perhaps even more important, he now really enjoys reading. Both he and Mary have been doing a great deal of science, including collecting and identifying many insects, leaves, and flowers. Mary also finds she has more time to pursue special interests in math and music without neglecting her studies in other areas. In short, we are very pleased with our home school and are looking forward to beginning our second year. We are glad we live in a state that has a balanced home schooling law.

If the home schooling law is reasonable, you could say something like:

The law has worked well since it was enacted. It holds home schoolers accountable and ensures that the compulsory school attendance law can be applied to home schoolers. There is no evidence that any further regulation of home schoolers is necessary; in fact, increased regulation could be detrimental.

Or, if the home schooling law is unreasonable, you might say something like:

The law has not worked well since it was enacted. It has major problems and results in unfair treatment of home schoolers. There is strong evidence that this law should be changed because ...

If you have any questions about home education or would like more information from us, please let us know.

Sincerely yours,

Your signature

Your full name

209

Among the topics you may want to discuss with your legislators are:

--How well or poorly the existing home schooling law or legal situation is working for you.

--What is happening with home schoolers when they return to conventional schools and go on to college, work, or the military.

--The idea that any home schooling law should balance the state's rights to ensure that children do not grow up to become a burden on the state, parents' rights to choose an education for their child that is consistent with their beliefs and principles, and a child's rights to a quality education consistent with her needs and abilities. Explain how well or poorly your state is balancing these rights. (For more details about these rights, see pp. 221-222.)

--Whether there is any demonstrated need for home schooling parents to be held accountable for their children's education through statutes and whether your state is dealing with this issue fairly.

A review of other sections of this handbook should give you more details on these points and ideas for other topics to discuss. You may also find it helpful to ask your legislators whether they have questions or concerns about home schooling. Chapter 15, "Common Questions about Home Schooling," may help you prepare to answer these questions. Offer to send your legislators more information if they are interested and to find out about questions they ask that you cannot answer. Ask your legislators for their support on issues that are important to you. Inquire about their position on these issues and on home schooling in general. (It may be important to realize, however, that most legislators do not invest a great deal of time on any single issue, especially if it is not up for consideration in their specific committee or for a general vote.)

CONTACTING YOUR LEGISLATOR TO DISCUSS A SPECIFIC BILL

When you hear about a bill relating to home schooling, it is time to act, whether or not you have already contacted your legislators. First, check with other home schoolers in your district to be sure you are working together and not against each other. Get a copy of the bill by writing or calling your legislator or the legislative 800 number. You may also request a free copy of the Blue or Red Book, a helpful reference book on your state government. For a discussion of this book and other legislative resources, see pp. 128-130.

After reading the bill, write or call your legislators. If writing, you may want to begin by identifying yourself, your work, community, position, etc. State your concern or request, identifying the bill by number and general subject. Thank your legislator for any previous help (including sending you a copy of the bill, if he did). State the main arguments to support your position factually and briefly. It is fine to indicate how the bill would affect your family but even better if you can indicate how it will affect others as well. Assume that your letter will be read and acted upon. Be reasonable and courteous, and do not use threats or exaggerated or misleading information. Ask your legislator to tell you his views on the bill and to notify you when a hearing is scheduled. Close with a note of thanks and your full name. If your legislator responds favorably, send a letter of appreciation.

SAMPLE LETTER TO A LEGISLATOR CONCERNING A SPECIFIC BILL

Your street address
City, state, zip
Date

The Honorable (full name)
Member of Assembly/House or Senate
State Capitol Building
City, state, zip

Sir (or Madam):

Thank your for sending me a copy of bill number 000, concerning _____. I am writing to ask you to work for and vote for this bill. The main reasons I support this bill are _____.

or

Thank you for sending me a copy of bill number 000, concerning _____. I am writing to share my concerns about this bill and to ask you to work and vote against it. The main reasons I oppose this bill are _____.

Please send me your views on this issue. If you have any questions or want further information, let me know.

Please inform me when a hearing is scheduled on this bill.

Thank you for your consideration of this matter.

Sincerely yours,

Your signature

Your full name

If you want to talk with your legislator, you can call the office or call the legislative 800 number and ask to have her call you. Plan your call before you dial; list the issues you want to cover and rehearse if you like. When you call, identify yourself. If your legislator is busy or not available, you may have to talk with an aide. Be courteous. Give the specific reason for your call and say you would like her to work for (or against) the bill. Stick to the facts. If your legislator or the aide disagrees, listen carefully to determine the real objection. Explore disagreements but do not argue. If she asks a question you cannot answer, offer to find out and call back. Ask your legislator if she will work for and vote for (or against) the bill. Close with a thank you.

Remember that legislators are waiting to hear from their constituents and that your letter or call can make a difference. It is unusual for a state legislator to get more than 5 to 8 letters on any given issue, so it does not take many letters to make an impression on him.

PARTICIPATING IN A HEARING

Hearings are held to provide information and perspective on pending legislation for legislators and for the public record. Your attendance is very important, whether you speak or not. In most states you can simply register for or against the bill on the form provided at the hearing. The following suggestions are for people who want to speak at a hearing.

Learn as much as you can about the bill as soon as it is introduced. You can get a copy from your legislator or by contacting the appropriate central office that distributes bills. Find out the names of the members of the committee that will be holding the hearing. The Blue or Red Book can be very useful in helping you understand more about the supporters of the bill and the committee members who will be dealing with it. Contact your state political home schooling organization and other home schoolers for their ideas. Find out who else is testifying and coordinate the subjects each of you will cover or decide on a few representatives from your group to testify. Review your draft testimony with others. Verify the date, time, and place for the hearing by calling the aide to the committee and/or the legislative agency that provides such information.

During the hearing, address the committee chairperson and its members as "Mr./Ms./Mrs./Miss Chairperson and Members of the Committee." Thank them for holding the hearing and for inviting or allowing you to speak. Be polite and respectful. Make your points briefly but with enough detail and emphasis to be understood and remembered. You may want to explain why home schooling is important to you and your children and how the current law is working, either positively or negatively. Do not attack public or other private schools. Time limits for speakers will be determined by the number of people who want to speak and the length of the hearing. Plan to speak for 5 to 10 minutes but be prepared to shorten your presentation if requested.

State that you are speaking only for yourself, unless you have been explicitly authorized to speak for a support group or other organization. To promote unity among home schoolers and to help ensure that you remain united with other home schoolers in legislative battles, avoid highlighting either your personal credentials (degrees, teacher certification, etc.) or your use of standardized tests or other standards of acceptability related to conventional schools. Such references may lead committee members to conclude either that all home schoolers should have these credentials or follow these practices and/or that home schoolers would not object to the state's requiring such credentials or practices.

Be prepared to answer questions from committee members and to respond to testimony from speakers who disagree with you and are critical of home schooling. You may want to prepare by discussing possible questions with other home schoolers and/or reading Chapter 15, "Common Questions about Home Schooling."

Since hearings are public meetings, the information you give, including answers to questions, may become a matter of record and may be used by the committee and others in developing a position on an issue. Therefore, it is a good idea to give a written copy of your testimony to the chairperson before or after your presentation and also to keep a copy for your records. It may prove useful if your testimony later becomes a matter of debate or is forgotten or not used. Include on the written copy the name of the committee holding the hearing; the bill number and topic; the date, time, and location of the hearing; and your name and address.

CHAPTER 22

HOME SCHOOLING WITHOUT A HOME SCHOOLING LAW

Home schoolers living in a state which does not have a law which specifically covers home schooling should seriously consider the option of continuing without one. Among the points worth pondering:

--Home schooling laws do not necessarily solve problems for home schoolers. Basically each home schooler has to take responsibility for his home school, regardless of the laws that exist or do not exist. Parents want what is best for their child and do not need a law to motivate them to do a good job of home schooling. On the other hand, the best law in the world will not prevent a local school official from making unreasonable and illegal demands on home schoolers, and then it is up to the parents to stand up for their rights whether these have been codified in a specific home schooling law or not.

--The fewer the legal restrictions that exist, the greater the flexibility that home schoolers have to figure out the way of educating their child that works best for them and the better chance they have of coming to a workable arrangement with a reasonable school official, if necessary. Even with a good law, it takes a lot of effort to deal with an unreasonable official.

--Many aspects of life are not regulated by law, do not need to be, and in fact benefit from the absence of statutory regulation. Basically laws are a middle choice as a way of enabling a society to function. They are less satisfactory and more cumbersome and tedious than approaches such as common agreement, mutual respect, cooperation, and tradition, but they have obvious advantages over approaches such as coercion and brute force.

--Ideally home schooling would be so widely understood and accepted as an educational alternative that laws would not be required either to protect home schoolers or to regulate them. In fact, this is how traditional home schools existed until compulsory school attendance laws were passed, which was not until after 1850.

--Until a few years ago, home schooling laws served two functions. First, they asserted the legality of home schooling and guaranteed parents' right to home school under certain conditions. Second, they gave the state some means of regulating home schooling. Now, however, few people question the right of home schoolers to exist or even consider attempting to outlaw home schooling altogether. The focus of the debate has shifted to how home schools should be regulated. This means that home schoolers have little to gain and much to lose through home schooling laws. The main thing a home schooling law could offer home schoolers now would be protection from unreasonable regulation by a government official. However, it takes a lot of effort to enforce such a law when dealing with an unreasonable official, and reasonable ones do not cause problems.

--Once home schoolers enter the political arena, they have to stay there. It would be extremely difficult to get rid of a home schooling law once it was passed, and once the principle of state regulation of home schooling is established, there is a continual threat of increasing regulation.

--Once a bill is introduced, it may be amended at any time up to the point of final passage. (Actually, in states which allow the governor to veto part of a bill and sign the rest, a bill can be significantly changed until it has been signed.) This makes it very difficult to control the legislative process, and what starts out as a reasonable home schooling bill may well end up including some highly objectionable requirements and regulations.

--In states without specific home school laws, it might also be wise for home schoolers not to get involved in litigation since it often leads to changes in laws and/or regulations.

CHAPTER 23

ARGUMENTS THAT SUPPORT
REASONABLE HOME SCHOOLING LAWS

As the previous chapter showed, there are many practical reasons why it is in the best interest of both home schoolers and society as a whole not to have laws dealing specifically with home schooling. In fact, it can be argued that any law is at best a compromise, that it would be better to operate a society on the basis of consensus and common agreement. Certainly for home schoolers the most reasonable approach would be no law at all but rather a general agreement that parents want what is best for their children, that children want to learn and are good at it, and that home is a good place to learn. However, this chapter exists because we do not live in an ideal world. Many states have home schooling laws that would be very difficult if not impossible to remove from the statutes. Sometimes the pressure for a law is so strong that home schoolers have to abandon their efforts to prevent the passage of a law and instead focus on getting the most reasonable law they can. Nevertheless, while reading this chapter, remember that ideally there would be no home schooling statutes as such.

Among the practical uses for a chapter such as this are the following:

--Home schoolers with a clear understanding of rational arguments that support reasonable home schooling laws are in a much better position to deal calmly, reasonably, effectively, confidently, and not defensively with challenges to their decision to home school, whether these challenges come from a restless child who misses the social activity of school, well-meaning friends and relatives, local school personnel, the state legislature, or their own internal doubts and fatigue. The educational establishment has done a frighteningly effective job of convincing people that conventional schooling is essential and good. Rare is the home schooler who does not benefit from a review of arguments that support the right and freedom of parents to home school.

--Home schoolers who are planning ways to gain public support for home schooling or developing a strategy for a legislative battle will find it helpful to have a clear idea of the principles that support their plans for action. Their strategy will be determined in part by which arguments will be most effective in a given situation. Sometimes this applies even if the arguments are not directly and specifically expressed to supporters or opponents.

--People who are open-minded on the subject of home schooling may become supporters when presented with well-reasoned arguments.

--Fact sheets or white papers on home schooling can be effective during a legislative battle. Even people who refuse to accept the validity of the arguments will sometimes admit that the existence of such a well reasoned fact sheet shows that home schoolers can express themselves well and need to be taken seriously.

--Other sections of this book present reasons for avoiding court cases when possible (see pp. 144-147). However, when such cases are unavoidable, the following arguments may be of value.

ELEMENTS OF A REASONABLE HOME SCHOOLING LAW (IF ONE IS ABSOLUTELY UNAVOIDABLE)

If a home schooling law is simply unavoidable, a reasonable law should protect the rights of the state, of parents, and of children.

(1) Rights of the state: Courts have ruled that the state has a right to ensure that children do not grow up to be a burden on the state and that the compulsory school attendance law is enforced. (Remember that compulsory school attendance laws require that a child attend an educational program, but such laws do not and cannot prescribe the nature of the program or dictate the outcome. Therefore, parents may need to show that their child is attending an educational program, but they should not be required to demonstrate the outcome of this attendance.)

(2) Rights of parents: Parents have the right to secure for their children an education consistent with their beliefs and principles. The state may not have a monopoly in education and cannot demand a uniform education for all. This means parents are protected from unreasonable state regulation and interference.

(3) Children's rights include the right

--to attend a quality educational program consistent with each child's needs and abilities.

--to have their education determined by their abilities and needs and not by the needs of professionals to be employed as specialists in day care, early childhood education, special education, and/or social work.

--to learn at the pace best suited to each child, free from harmful competition and comparisons.

--not to be forced to take standardized tests (which can often be unfair, biased, and inappropriate, and which dictate

221

curriculum) and not be labeled and tracked, especially at an early age.

--to be a member of a family which is supported by the larger community and not torn apart by it.

--to be helped and supported by parents and others.

--to be treated as an individual human of value and not as a cog in a factory modeled economic machine.

ARGUMENTS THAT SUPPORT REASONABLE HOME SCHOOLING LAWS AND OPPOSE UNREASONABLE ONES

An extensive list of arguments is given here, with some inevitable repetition of basic points so nuances and subtleties can be included and so each section will be nearly self-contained. Legal arguments are listed first because home schoolers must deal with them so often. However, as the authors, we do not think that legal arguments are the most compelling or effective way of supporting home schooling. We strongly caution you against relying too heavily on them. Instead, select the arguments that are most applicable to your specific situation and add your own. Many of these are based on common sense and a willingness to question current educational practices and the assumptions on which they are based. The arguments are organized into several categories; in reality they overlap and interrelate.

LEGAL ARGUMENTS

(1) Constitutional arguments. The U.S. Constitution does not specifically mention education. However, rights of citizens which apply to home schooling parents and children are guaranteed by the first, fourth, fifth, ninth, and fourteenth amendments to the Constitution. In general terms, these provisions are:

--The U.S. Constitution does guarantee rights that are important to home schoolers (as well as all other citizens, of course). The first amendment guarantees freedom of religion, speech, and the press, and the rights of assembly and petition.

--The fourth amendment states, "The right of the people to be secure in their persons, houses, papers, and effects, against unreasonable searches and seizures, shall not be violated, but upon probable cause." In other words, the state must have reasonable cause or evidence in order to come into your house or threaten your person or insist that you answer questions. (See discussion of fifth amendment below for more information on due process since establishing probable cause is done through the due process.)

--The fifth amendment provides protection from being compelled to testify against yourself ("taking the fifth"), the right to trial by jury, and the right not to "be deprived of life, liberty, or property, without due process of law." The right to due process has been used to protect personal liberties. (This right is strengthened and given more authority under the fourteenth amendment.)

--The ninth amendment says that there are some rights that are retained by the people even though they are not listed in the Constitution. This amendment is important for people who want to reclaim rights that the state has usurped by custom and even by statute, since they can argue that the state had no constitutional basis for taking away these rights in the first place. Under this amendment, courts have recently upheld parental rights in education and rights to privacy.

--Section 1 of the fourteenth amendment provides civil rights that are very important to an individual, especially anyone in a minority position. First, "no state shall make or enforce any law which shall abridge the privileges or immunities of citizens of the United States." In other words, state laws may not take away fundamental privileges (rights and liberties) guaranteed by the U.S. Constitution. Second, "nor shall any state deprive any person of life, liberty, or property, without due process of law." While this provision seems to repeat the language of the fifth amendment, here it is established that an individual state may not do this. For example, a state may not pass laws that deny a parent's constitutional right to choose for his child an education consist with the parent's beliefs and principles. Third, "nor deny to any person within its jurisdiction the equal protection of the laws." Each individual has equal rights and liberties under the law. Home schoolers can use this in dealings with public school officials. It could be argued, for example, that public school officials cannot legally deny home schoolers access to public schools merely because they are home schoolers. Nor can they legally require of home schoolers more than is required of other students in order to be enrolled or placed in a given grade.

(2) Case law. Rulings by the U.S. Supreme Court and federal, state, and local courts interpret and expand upon the Constitution. Among the most important for home schoolers are the U.S. Supreme Court cases *Pierce v. Society of Sisters* (268 U.S. 510 [1925]) and *Farrington v. Tokushige* (273 U.S. 284 [1927]) in which the court ruled that parents have a right to secure for their children an education consistent with their principles and beliefs and that the state may not have a monopoly in education.

Home schoolers who are involved in serious legislative or court battles are strongly encouraged to study these in greater depth. More detailed information about both Constitutional arguments and case law can be found in John Holt's *Teach Your Own*, pp. 271-324, and John W. Whitehead and Wendell R. Bird's *Home Education and Constitutional Liberties*. And of course there is no substitute for reading the original documents themselves.

(3) Common law. This is a system based on practice, court decisions, and customs and usage rather than on statutes. Some of the legal maxims or principles which are so widely accepted that they do not need to be written down and can be applied to home schooling in the United States are:

--"Innocent until proven guilty." This means the burden of proof is on the state to prove an individual's guilt. Thus although the state has authority to ensure that children do not grow up to be a burden on the state, the courts have found that parents have rights in education which the state may not violate. Home schooling parents should not need to prove themselves innocent (by meeting certification requirements or showing that their curriculum is substantially equivalent to that of a public school or having their children tested) as a condition for exercising their parental rights in education. Laws which require such proof have been significantly reduced through courts and state legislatures, particularly during the past 15 years. (However, within the past three or four years home schooling legislative and regulatory changes in states such as New York, Pennsylvania, and New Hampshire suggest a change toward greater regulation once again.)

--Rights of a minority. A person cannot be prosecuted or forced to abandon his principles or practices just because the majority of the people do not agree with him or choose his approach. The fact that home schoolers are choosing an approach to education that is different from that chosen by the majority of Americans today is not grounds for prosecution.

--Civil liberties. Everyone, including home schoolers, is entitled to fundamental civil liberties, some of which are described in the Bill of Rights and some of which are common law. Therefore, a law which violates the civil liberties of a home schooler is wrong and should not be passed.

--"Hard cases make bad law." In other words, a law designed to take care of the worst possible hypothetical case is almost certain to be long, difficult to enforce, and more likely to prevent good people from doing good than bad people from doing bad. It is unfair and solves nothing to punish conscientious home schoolers by passing an unnecessarily restrictive law that does not solve the problem of high risk children anyway. Such a law would damage the effectiveness of good home schools.

(4) Limitations of the compulsory school attendance law: Home schooling laws are based on compulsory school attendance laws. (If there were no attendance laws, the state would have no

basis for regulating home schooling; home schoolers could simply not attend school.) However, it is extremely important to realize that compulsory school attendance laws require attendance, not education. The law can and does require that children attend an educational program, and children can and do comply, and this can be demonstrated and enforced. But the law cannot and does not prescribe a specific educational program or dictate the outcome. In other words, the law requires that a child attend, but it does not and cannot require that the child learn anything from the program. There is no general agreement on what it means to be "educated" or on how one proves someone is "educated." Even to begin to set definitions and requirements would quickly violate individual rights and freedoms. When parents have tried to sue a conventional school for failing to educate their children, courts have consistently ruled that schools cannot be held accountable if children attending them fail to become educated. Education simply cannot be legislated, and it cannot be legally required. This fact has important ramifications, beginning with strong limitations on the state's ability to dictate the specifics of the curriculum or content of educational programs.

LOGICAL ARGUMENTS

(1) Laws that regulate home schools are basically unnecessary. The experiences of thousands of parents and children have shown that parents are very capable of educating their children at home. There is no substantial evidence that the thousands of home schoolers throughout the country are having any significant problems. In addition, thousands of formerly home schooled children have entered or re-entered conventional schools without significant problems, showing that their home schooling experience did not handicap them or make them unable to handle the work done in conventional schools. To be sure, some of these home schoolers have been regulated in varying degrees. But there is no evidence that there are more problems in states with fewer or no regulations.

(2) There is no home schooling law or regulation that would improve home schools. Home schooling works because people (both adults and children) are well equipped to learn if given a chance. Home schools work because they are small enough and flexible enough to meet the needs of individual children and allow them to use their strengths. They work because parents care about their children and want what is best for them. People do not become loving and caring parents or conscientious home schoolers because there are laws that require them to do this.

(3) Regulations can be harmful to home schools and limit their effectiveness. Regulations that interfere with the alternative nature of home schools or that limit their flexibility make it more difficult for home schools to be effective and to meet the needs of their students.

(4) It is commonly understood and widely accepted by people who think seriously about it that parents are responsible (practically and legally) for seeing that their children have an appropriate opportunity to become educated. Some parents choose to delegate this responsibility to a conventional school while others (called home schoolers) decide to fulfill their responsibility directly themselves. If the basic responsibility for a child's education lies with his parents, one can certainly ask what basis the state has for attempting to regulate that education.

(5) Some proposed home schooling laws and regulations imply that parents cannot be trusted to teach their children. However, parents can in fact be trusted because:

(a) Home schooling is a big responsibility and a lot of work. It is not something parents undertake lightly. Free public schools are a very readily available alternative for parents who do not want to be strongly involved with their children through home schooling.

(b) People (both parents and children) are well equipped to learn if given a chance.

227

(c) Some argue that home schooled children are too strongly influenced by their parents and too isolated. However, children are strongly influenced by their parents whether they are home schooled or not. Home schoolers are active in their neighborhoods, communities, and various groups, and home schooled children interact with a wide variety of people of differing ages and backgrounds.

(6) It is widely held that parents have a stronger influence on children who attend schools than do the schools. For example, when schools are criticized for not educating children, they often defend themselves by saying that they are unable to overcome the influence of the children's parents and home life. The central importance of parents to education has been documented in recent summaries of educational research spanning the past 20 years. (See p. 99.) Since parents are the strongest influence in a child's education whether she attends a conventional school or a home school, how does it make sense for the state to try to regulate parents who are home schooling?

HISTORICAL ARGUMENTS

Throughout human history, the vast majority of people have been educated at home by their parents. In fact, many people, unfortunately labeled "primitives," have had the good fortune to live rich and full lives without anyone telling them they were being "educated" in the process. The first compulsory school attendance laws in the United States were not passed until after 1850, and it was not until after World War II that all states had such laws. Although home schooling is often labeled "new and different," it is really a very old, traditional, tried-and-true approach to education that works very well.

Some people argue that "times have changed" and that formal education is required in today's highly technological society. However, times are changing so fast that what is most important is that people learn how to learn, how to be flexible and handle

228

change, and how to solve problems. Home schools are especially good environments for acquiring these abilities.

PRACTICAL ARGUMENTS

(1) Home schooling works. It works well for a wide variety of children who begin home schooling at various ages for different reasons. It can be especially important for children who have difficulty learning in conventional schools, including children who have been labeled as "learning disabled," "slow learners," etc. Because home schooling provides such a workable alternative, it should be readily available without unreasonable regulation, especially since it is clearly a better approach to education for some children than a conventional school.

(2) Home schooling provides a wide range of learning opportunities and ways of learning. Because of this, home schools prevent the development of learning difficulties in many children and are very helpful to some children who are not primarily skilled at learning through reading and writing, which are the main approaches to learning offered by most conventional schools.

(3) Home schools provide an excellent opportunity to learn about how children learn. By their nature, home schools can focus on learning and do not need to deal with concerns of discipline and classroom management that are often the first concerns of conventional teachers. (If a teacher cannot control a class, how can he teach?) The flexible, many-faceted, alternative character of home schools means that they offer a rich opportunity for children to learn in many different ways, and for interested people to observe this and learn from watching the children.

(4) Home schools save taxpayers money. Every child who does not attend a public school saves the cost of his education.

(5) No matter how well educated a parent is when she begins home schooling, she inevitably learns a great deal from the

229

experience. Home schooling is an educational experience for the whole family, providing important learning benefits for a whole range of people.

(6) Neither lay persons nor professional educators can agree on the best way to educate a child. In the absence of such agreement, a range of alternatives, including home schooling, needs to be permitted and encouraged.

MORAL ARGUMENTS

(1) Our society has an obligation to provide each child the education best suited to him. Since children vary widely in their needs, abilities, interests, and talents, a wide range of alternative approaches to education, including home schooling, must be available, and families must be able to choose the best alternative for each child. Also, for home schools to function as true alternatives, they must be free from unreasonable restrictions, some of which would make them similar to conventional schools.

(2) A society that believes in freedom of thought and freedom of belief must allow parents to choose for their children an education consistent with their principles and beliefs and must allow people to choose alternative approaches to education without unreasonable regulation.

(3) The family is the fundamental unit of any society. Home schooling strengthens families; opposition to home schooling and unreasonable regulation of home schooling weaken families. Parents who choose to home school are choosing one way of taking seriously their responsibilities for their children. They deserve the support of the larger community in which they live.

RELIGIOUS ARGUMENTS

Religious beliefs and arguments are very important to many home schoolers and provide very strong support for home schooling. Under our federal constitution the state may not pass any law or engage in practices that would either establish a religion or interfere with a person's religion, including a parent's instructing her child in religion. However, specific religious arguments that support home schooling are not presented here because they are understandably personal and vary widely.

GENERAL ARGUMENTS AGAINST UNREASONABLE HOME SCHOOLING LAWS

(1) Home schooling regulations are generally intended to make home schools more like conventional schools. This seriously interferes with the flexibility home schools need to operate effectively, it ruins their ability to serve as effective alternatives to conventional schools, and it unnecessarily restricts their functioning. These regulations also may be unconstitutional since the courts have ruled that the state may not have a monopoly in education and attempts to make home schools like conventional schools advance the public school monopoly in education.

(2) "Hard cases make bad law." In other words, a law designed to take care of the worst possible hypothetical case is almost certain to be long, difficult to enforce, and more likely to prevent good people from doing good than bad people from doing bad. It is unfair and solves nothing to punish conscientious home schoolers by passing an unnecessarily restrictive law that does not solve the problem of high risk children anyway. Such a law would also damage the effectiveness of good home schools.

(3) Home schooling regulations are unnecessary and therefore a waste of the time, energy, and money of home schoolers, public officials, and taxpayers. Even if there were a very few home schoolers who were not doing a good job, their problems would

not be prevented or solved by a restrictive home schooling law. Instead they could be handled by other existing laws such as those covering child abuse and neglect.

(4) Home schools cannot be improved by restrictive legislation; learning, education, and parental commitment cannot be legislated. But home schools can certainly be harmed by legislation.

ARGUMENTS AGAINST SPECIFIC HOME SCHOOLING REGULATIONS

The most common restrictions on home schooling can be grouped in the categories shown below. The general arguments listed above can be used against all of these restrictions, and there are also specific arguments that can be used in each case. (As a general strategy, it is better for a small minority group like home schoolers to try to prevent the introduction of any legislation and to oppose specific proposals when they are introduced. Home schoolers differ widely in what they consider acceptable regulations, and many feel that no regulation is acceptable. If home schoolers do come to some agreement and support the introduction of legislation they feel would be acceptable, they run the serious risk that it will be amended before passage and end up dramatically different from what they originally supported.)

ARGUMENTS AGAINST REQUIRING THAT HOME SCHOOLS BE "SUBSTANTIALLY EQUIVALENT" TO PUBLIC SCHOOLS

(1) This requirement would cost Americans one of their most fundamental rights, the right to think and learn freely without unnecessary interference. To preserve these rights, we need to preserve the distinctions between public and private schools including home schools.

(2) This would dangerously increase the strength and power of the educational bureaucracy, which already has nearly a strangle-hold on American education. There must be alternatives to the public school system, and home schools are a good one.

(3) As explained above, constitutional law has made it clear that the state may not have a monopoly in education. Therefore, this requirement may well be unconstitutional because it would move toward giving the state such a monopoly.

(4) The compulsory school attendance laws require attendance, not education. For more details, see pp. 225-226.

(5) This requirement makes no sense. Neither lay persons nor professional educators can agree on the one best method for educating a child. Many people have serious questions and reservations about contemporary American public schools. What reasonable basis is there for requiring that home schools be like them?

(6) This requirement would seriously interfere with home schools, which need flexibility in order to function effectively. It would also be a terrible waste, because it would needlessly limit home schools and prevent them from trying new approaches to education, using unconventional approaches that work, and taking full advantage of the many opportunities that are available to small groups of learners working together in the real world.

(7) Such a requirement would be essentially impossible to enforce. Individual public schools vary widely, and there is no consensus as to what specific criteria a public school must meet. Without clear criteria, it would be impossible to say that a home school was equivalent to a public school. Also, home schools are by their nature and composition very different from public schools. They have fewer students, offer a much wider range of learning opportunities, do not have classroom management or group discipline problems similar to those of a conventional school, etc. Therefore it is very difficult to compare home schools and public schools--the old "apples and oranges" problem.

ARGUMENTS AGAINST REQUIRING REVIEW AND APPROVAL OF HOME SCHOOL CURRICULUMS BY PUBLIC SCHOOL OFFICIALS

(1) Given the training, experience, and bias of a public school official, she most likely would consider home schools acceptable only if they were very similar to public schools. Therefore, this is another way of stating the requirement that home schools become "substantially equivalent" to public schools. Arguments (1) through (6) under "substantially equivalent" above also apply here.

(2) It is unrealistic and inappropriate to have public school officials judge home schools because

(a) Most officials have limited understanding of the major differences between home schools and public schools.

(b) Many public school officials see home schools as a threat to the educational system to which they have made a commitment and on which they are dependent for their jobs and careers. Their sense of self-interest and self-preservation gives them a very negative, biased, and unfair perspective on home schools.

(c) Public school officials have been trained not to look at individuals but to manage and control children through standardization and routinization. This does not equip them to understand or fairly assess home schools.

(d) Public schools obviously do not have the answers to how to educate all children. But what happens if an official is confronted with a home schooler who is learning by means of an approach that is very different from that of the public schools?

(e) In many cases in which school officials have been given authority to review and approve home schools, they have been arbitrary and unfair.

234

(3) Some people argue that since review and approval should not be troublesome to conscientious home schoolers, it should be required "just to be sure" that home schoolers are getting a good education. However, for the reasons outlined above and others, review and approval <u>would</u> be troublesome to conscientious home schoolers.

ARGUMENTS AGAINST REQUIRING PORTFOLIO ASSESSMENTS OF HOME SCHOOLED CHILDREN

(1) Most of the above arguments against review and approval also apply.

(2) Assessments put pressure on children, invade their privacy, limit their freedom of exploration and expression, and force them to focus on products rather than process, on results rather than learning.

ARGUMENTS AGAINST REQUIRING INDEPENDENT ASSESSMENT OF HOME SCHOOLS BY PERSONS NOT ASSOCIATED WITH THE PUBLIC SCHOOLS

(1) Some people contend that home schoolers should not object to assessment by non-public school persons. For example, it is sometimes suggested that a professional (such as a psychologist, minister, or social worker) or a home schooling organization could take responsibility for this. However, professionals would generally apply criteria and standards similar to their own experience or the requirements of conventional schools. How is this justified when home schools are an alternative to this experience and set of practices? Assessments by other home schoolers or by a state-wide home school organization that is recognized by the state as an accrediting body would also not be effective since such judgments are very difficult to make without

235

imposing one's own approach. An outsider gets a very limited picture of a home school and cannot accurately judge it.

(2) Any time assessments are made there is the expectation that something will be done with the results. Assessors are not working primarily as constructive consultants; the presumption is that home schoolers may be doing something that needs to be corrected. Assessors tend to record their judgments with at least three things in mind: First, how can I make this somewhat unique situation comprehensible to persons outside the home school? Second, how do I justify the home school in the eyes of others? Third, how will my assessment of this home school affect my reputation and professional standing? Such intervention and oversight are not healthy for a home school and have not been demonstrated to be necessary or effective.

(3) Even if the assessments are kept by the home schooling family and not turned over to officials, they serve as the basis for potential prosecution. The assessors and those assessed understand this implicitly if not explicitly.

(4) This type of assessment requires home schoolers to prove that they are doing a good job, even though there is no evidence that they are not. This violates the principle of innocent until proven guilty.

(5) Such regulation assumes that experts or professionals generally can better determine whether a parent is understanding and attending to a child's education than the parent can. This simply is not true. Such professionals can determine whether the home school fits their expectations, but such expectations may be very inappropriate to a home school.

ARGUMENTS AGAINST STATE-MANDATED STANDARDIZED TESTING

(1) In order for a child to have a reasonable chance of doing well on a standardized test, he must have been exposed to the

curriculum. As was pointed out above, this is inappropriate, unwise, and probably unconstitutional.

(2) Standardized tests are fraught with difficulties. They do not measure what they purport to measure; instead they measure only how good an individual is at taking a test. They have been proven to be culturally biased and to discriminate against women, minorities, creative thinkers, and those who do not have the same values or experience as the test-makers.

(3) Despite the severe limitations, defects, and unfairness of standardized tests, the results are taken seriously by test-giver and test-taker alike. Too often one unfair and erroneous test can result in a child's being labeled "learning disabled" or seriously limited in some other way. Effects can be life-long in terms of lost opportunities, self-confidence, and self-esteem.

(4) Numerous studies have criticized standardized tests and cautioned against their use. Most recently, a report issued by the National Commission on Testing and Public Policy in May, 1990, recommended significantly curtailing standardized tests in elementary schools and strongly limiting their use by colleges and employers. This report is based on a three year study of scholarly reports on the subject.

(5) Standardized tests interfere with learning in a wide variety of ways. They force a child to focus on oversimplified answers rather than on questions and problem solving. They often interfere with the direction a child's learning is taking. They are a vote of no confidence; you do not test someone on something you are confident she knows. Taking such a test can be a frightening, intimidating experience for a child.

ARGUMENTS AGAINST REQUIRING THAT HOME SCHOOL TEACHERS BE CERTIFIED

(1) Educational policy makers are seriously questioning teacher certification. See p. 97 for more information about this. Many private schools have never required teacher certification. Why should home schoolers be subjected to a flawed practice that many conventional schools have never adopted and others are attempting to abandon?

(2) Experienced home schoolers realize that they do not need to know everything their child wants to learn. In fact, many enjoy sometimes learning with their child, sharing the excitement of discovery and setting an important example of life-long learning.

(3) Family background and parental participation in a child's education consistently have been shown to have more to do with a child's learning than any other factor, including teacher training and specialization. (See p. 99.)

(4) One major goal of teacher certification is to prepare a person to control and manage a group of children and work with all of them at once. Since home schooling parents do not face such a situation, they do not need and would not benefit from much of what is involved in conventional certification.

(5) The qualities that are important in a home schooling parent (concern for children, love of learning, willingness to try new ideas and approaches to learning, etc.) are not qualities that can be tested for, evaluated, or legislated. With free public schools so readily available, it is highly unlikely that parents would choose to home school if they were not willing to work hard and did not feel they were qualified.

(6) If you cannot trust parents who want to educate their own children and are willing to do the hard work involved in undertaking this serious responsibility, whom can you trust?

COMMUNICATING THESE ARGUMENTS TO LEGISLATORS, POLICY MAKERS, AND OTHERS

Often when fighting a legislative battle, presenting testimony at a hearing, etc., it is helpful to prepare a fact sheet or white paper that includes facts and arguments that support home schoolers' positions and counter those of the opposition. Some of the following suggestions may be helpful; remember that you are the best judge of what to do in the specific situation in which you are involved.

(1) Select the arguments that are most appropriate to the issue at hand and that are most likely to persuade your audience. If you are fighting to prevent the introduction of new or stronger regulations, point out that the current situation is working well, that there is no substantial evidence that home schoolers are a problem, and that greater regulation of home schools is unnecessary and would be harmful.

(2) Try to see the issue from the audience's perspective. Of course your interests and concerns are important to you, but you have a much better chance of getting the result you want if you can convince others that they will benefit from what you want. For example, you might include a section called "Why Our State Needs Thriving Home Schools" which points out that home schools provide a valuable alternative for children, help ensure that the state does not have a monopoly in education, save the taxpayers money, protect important rights and freedoms, etc.

(3) Avoid arguments that identify home schooling with a specific political party or faction. Home schooling is not a partisan issue, and allying yourself with one side will cost you important support from the other and divide home schoolers.

(4) Do not attack the public schools. This will only cloud the issue; make school people, legislators, and the general public feel defensive; and inadvertently establish the public schools as the criterion by which a home school should be judged.

(5)   Balance length and thoroughness.   Include all the important points but remember that often the longer a paper is, the less likely it is to be read.   One solution is to present a brief summary at the beginning followed by one or more pages of supporting details and facts with the important points in bold type and/or underlined.   Sometimes a question and answer format works well, with questions in bold type.

(6) Make the sheet attractive.   Choose a readable type style and leave some empty space so the sheet does not look crowded or overwhelming.   Consider the attractiveness and uniqueness of using colored paper, but be sure to pick a light color on which print can easily be read.   Proof read carefully.   If the sheet is coming from an organization, include its name, address, and phone number in a prominent place.   If appropriate, give a contact for further information.

CHAPTER 24

OTHER LAWS

Home schoolers obviously are affected by laws which apply to all students. Specific provisions of these laws may make home schooling easier or more difficult. This chapter presents a brief discussion of some of these laws, including descriptions of their constructive and negative provisions and ideas for alternative ways of dealing with them. It may be helpful to give serious consideration to these options if your state is considering revising its laws in any of these areas.

COMPULSORY SCHOOL ATTENDANCE LAWS

Every state has a compulsory school attendance law. These laws have been upheld by numerous state and U.S. Supreme Court cases, on the grounds that the state has the right to see that citizens do not grow up to become a burden on the state. (At the same time it should be understood that the U. S. Constitution gives the states no authority in education. Nothing in the Constitution requires compulsory school attendance laws, and these laws have been passed relatively recently in our country, the first one not until after 1850.) The state's authority to enforce this law comes from the policing powers granted to the states by the U.S. Constitution.

Without compulsory school attendance laws, home schooling laws, regulations, or provisions would not be needed; home schoolers could simply say they were not going to school. Also, compulsory school attendance laws must cover home schoolers or they become unenforceable; anyone who did not want to attend school could simply say he was home schooling. Some people question the wisdom of having compulsory school attendance laws. They argue that we do not have the right to require that all children attend school, that there are other good ways for a child to grow up, and that people should be free to choose one of these alternatives. However, even people who oppose compulsory school attendance laws agree that there is essentially no chance of eliminating these laws at this point; the vast majority of people believe such laws are necessary. It seems more realistic to try to make compulsory school attendance laws as workable as possible. Some suggestions that may help:

--Remember that such laws require attendance but not education. For an explanation, see pp. 225-226.

--A compulsory school attendance law is more workable if it covers fewer years. Many parents are convinced that children benefit from not being required to begin school at too young an age, and there is strong evidence that children should not begin formal instruction until they are physically, neurologically, and emotionally ready. This varies with the individual but is often between 8 and 12 years of age. However, some states are considering changing their compulsory school attendance laws to require attendance at an earlier age. Home schoolers need to be aware of these possible changes and consider working to prevent them.

--A compulsory school attendance law is also more workable if it allows options and alternatives for older children. Some states accomplish this simply by requiring that children attend school only until age 14, 15, or 16. However, other states are extending the compulsory school attendance law to include older students; again, home schoolers should be alert for such a possibility.

Some states provide options for young people. For example, California allows 16 year olds to take an examination more difficult than the GED. Students who pass may move on to college, the military, or employment. In Minnesota, high school juniors and seniors may take courses at a public or private college or university. Tuition costs, books, and transportation are paid for with public school funds and the credits earned apply both to high school graduation and a college degree. Another possibility is to allow reasonable exceptions to the compulsory school attendance law for students who are interested in alternative approaches to education.

TRUANCY LAWS

Truancy laws follow logically from compulsory school attendance laws, so home schoolers need to be concerned about specific provisions of truancy laws in their state:

--The way truancy is defined and the kinds of absences that lead to a child's being classified as a truant. Laws also vary in how difficult they make it for parents to verify that a child's absence from school was legitimate.

--Penalties for truancy.

--The person responsible for determining truancy and enforcing the law. Are home schoolers under the supervision of the local school board, the superintendent, the truant officer, or someone at the state level?

PUBLIC SCHOOL RECORDS

False, misleading, and damaging information can be included in a child's school records and can cause serious problems. Parents of children who have attended a public school may want to gain access to these records and have them released or corrected. Obviously this is much easier to do when reasonable laws govern what may be included in pupil records and how parents may gain access to them.

SCHOOL CENSUS

Some states conduct a school census at regular intervals to aid them in planning for the future. However, sometimes census takers request more information than is legally allowed. Therefore, home schoolers who are concerned about protecting their child's privacy may want to find out what information is specifically required by law and refuse to give additional information.

IMMUNIZATION

Many states require that children be immunized against various diseases before attending a public school. Some states have extended these laws to cover private school students (including home schoolers). Reasonable laws waive the requirements for children whose parents object to immunization for one or more reasons including health, religion, and personal conviction. However, sometimes public officials do not inform parents about this provision of the law. Again, it is important for parents to know what the law requires and allows.

OTHER STATE REQUIREMENTS OF PUBLIC SCHOOL STUDENTS

Although home schoolers are not directly affected when new requirements (such as standardized curriculum, longer school days and school years, standardized testing) are placed on public school students, there may be an effort to extend these requirements to home schoolers as well.

244

REQUIREMENTS FOR PRIVATE SCHOOLS

Home school laws come in two forms. One is a law that applies specifically if not exclusively to home schoolers. The other is a law that applies to all private schools including home schools. In either case home schools are considered private as distinct from public. Therefore, home schoolers will be affected, either directly or indirectly, by any increase in state regulation of private schools, such as requirements that they hire only certified teachers, use standardized tests, institute certain graduation requirements, etc. Often people involved in private schools are good allies of home schoolers, although some private schools are so eager to become as much like public schools as possible that they do not share some concerns of home schoolers.

GED REGULATIONS

A home schooler who wishes to obtain a high school diploma by taking a GED (General Educational Development) examination is influenced by the pertinent laws and regulations. Controversy frequently surrounds the age at which a young person is allowed to take the exam. Home schoolers (and others interested in alternatives) argue that a student should be able to take the exam when she is ready, but schools often fear that too many people would choose a GED diploma rather than completing high school, so often one is not allowed to take the GED until age 18 or older. Some states require that a student do more than pass the exam; these extra requirements can cause complications. For more on the GED, see pp. 74-75.

245

CONCLUSION

Home schoolers are influenced by many laws in addition to specific home schooling laws. They are best able to protect themselves and maintain as many rights and options as possible when they are aware of specific requirements of such laws and of proposals to change them.

PART VI

MAKING THE BEST OF CURRENT LAW

CHAPTER 25

RESPONDING TO PUBLIC OFFICIALS

Some home schoolers are required to have regular contact with a school official; others feel calmer and more confident knowing they are prepared to deal with a public official should they be contacted unexpectedly. This chapter presents suggestions for dealing with both situations. It may also be helpful to read the ideas on reading and interpreting laws on pp. 197-201.

REQUIRED MEETINGS WITH SCHOOL OFFICIALS

Some states require that home schoolers meet with a school official. Some suggestions:

--Be very clear about exactly what the laws and regulations require. Reread them and take a copy to the meeting for reference. Remember that you do not have to do anything the law does not require, even if the official asks more of you in a threatening way or acts so warm and friendly that you feel you want to share more about your home school. In fact, if you do more than is required, you may set a precedent, and the official may expect other home schoolers to do as you have done. Also remember that your interpretation of the laws and regulations may differ from the official's interpretation, but that does not mean that his interpretation is more valid than yours or that you have to comply with his interpretation.

--Translate your child's learning activities into familiar terms the school official is expecting to hear. A child building with interlocking blocks is "using math manipulatives," a trip to the zoo or library is a "field trip," talking with a neighbor about the Depression is "history," cooking dinner is "home economics." Remember that you have to do the translating; few school officials are going to say, "You mentioned that your child resists working in her arithmetic book, but does she ever build with interlocking blocks? Well, those are what we call 'math manipulatives.'" You may want to review the ideas about the many ways children learn on pp. 32-37.

--If you have doubts or concerns about your home school, do not share them with the school official in the hopes that she might have some helpful suggestions or advice. This is more likely to get you into difficulty than to solve problems. It is much safer and more helpful to share your concerns with another home schooler.

--Before the meeting, you may want to talk with other home schoolers about their experiences and ideas, so you have a better idea of what to expect.

UNEXPECTED CONTACT FROM A PUBLIC OFFICIAL

AN OUNCE OF PREVENTION

Consider ways you can both reduce your chances of being contacted and strengthen your position if you are contacted. Some suggestions:

--Be thoroughly familiar with laws concerning home schooling, compulsory school attendance, and truancy. Have a copy available for quick reference. Many home schoolers feel more confident and better able to deal with school officials once they understand the broader legal context for home schooling. For further information on laws, see pp. 222-238.

--Think seriously about your compliance with the law. Most home schoolers comply with the law, even if they are not in complete agreement with it. Document your compliance. Suggestions for keeping records are on pp. 49-51.

--If your state has a home schooling law as distinct from a general private school law without specific reference to home schools, consider writing, calling, or visiting your local public school superintendent to inform him that you are home schooling and are in full compliance with the law (assuming of course that you are). Hopefully he will respond positively. If he begins asking inappropriate questions, be polite but remember you are complying with the law and do not need his approval. If necessary, end the phone conversation or leave the office, still being as polite as possible. Also, consider contacting the principal of your local school, using the same guidelines.

--Develop contacts in your local community who know you are doing a good job of home schooling and who could support you and possibly even testify on your behalf, if necessary. Possibilities include neighbors, librarians, friends who are involved in the public schools, members of your church, and adults with whom your child works, such as leaders of youth organizations.

--Meet your legislators. See pp. 206-213.

--Promote a positive image of home schooling in your community. See pp. 174-179.

--Consider seriously the way you present your home school to public officials and the general public. Many home schoolers find that it pays to be discreet. As far as possible, without compromising important principles, they appear as conventional as possible. They find that their home school is much more likely to be accepted and probably more accurately represented if they say, "Our children go to school at home," than if they say, "Our children don't go to school."

Home schoolers find they have to strike a balance between appearing conventional and taking advantage of the flexibility that is one of the important strengths of home schooling. Each parent has to consider the advantages of flexibility and freedom along with the risks of causing concern or arousing suspicion. Neighborhoods, school districts, and communities vary in their willingness to accept or tolerate "different" ideas like home schooling. Also, a family that is well known and accepted in the community may not need to be as cautious as a new family or one that has been involved in controversy unrelated to home schooling.

Home schoolers also face the question of the extent to which they should try to gain acceptance and recognition for their ability to do well what conventional schools do and the extent to which they should emphasize that home schools are different from conventional schools and thus offer children unique opportunities. Parents who encourage their children to pursue their own interests, learn at their own pace, and not worry about grade levels or standardized tests may particularly feel torn between the need to downplay these differences and the importance of sharing with others the exciting alternatives that make life and learning much more manageable, especially for children who may have trouble learning in a conventional school setting and for families who find it very stressful to try to duplicate what a conventional school does in their own home.

RESPONDING TO A WRITTEN REQUEST FROM AN OFFICIAL

Occasionally a school official writes to a home schooler with a request for more than is required by law. The home schooler can respond by explaining that she is in full compliance with the requirements of the law, that the official's request goes beyond these requirements, and that she will therefore not comply with the request. An example of such a letter, based on Wisconsin's home schooling law, is presented here. Letters of this type have been very successful because school officials often do not know the law themselves and/or are not accustomed to dealing with people who know their rights and act to protect them.

SAMPLE LETTER TO A SCHOOL OFFICIAL WHO REQUESTED DOCUMENTS

Your street address
City, state, zip
Date

Dr. or Mr. or Ms. (full name of official)
_____ School District
Street address
City, state, zip

Dear Dr. or Mr. or Ms. (last name):

I am writing in response to your letter dated _____, in which you requested_____.

This is to advise you that in accordance with the applicable laws governing a home-based private educational program, I have completed, signed, and sent form PI-1206 to the Department of Public Instruction and am in compliance with the laws referenced above. Further, there is no provision within the laws that grants to local public schools or the DPI monitoring responsibility or authority with regard to a home-based private educational program. This is clear from the laws themselves, from the legislative discussion and debate leading to the passage of the laws, from the Legislative Council's memorandum on the law, and from meetings and correspondence with the DPI and local public school officials concerning the administration of the laws.

We are aware that the attendance officer has authority under the <u>truancy</u> (as distinct from the daily attendance) provision of the attendance officer statutes (S. 118.16[b]) to initiate action when there is reasonable evidence of "intermittent attendance carried on for the purpose of defeating the intent of S. 118.15." However, your request does not concern a truancy matter.

After much discussion, the Wisconsin Legislature passed the "Definition of a Private School" law to ensure that home-based private educational programs were not subject to public school review or approval. This is in keeping with the educational rights of parents and the U.S. and Wisconsin Constitutions as well as the legislature's awareness of the importance of providing for and maintaining a distinction between public and private alternatives in education.

Therefore, I respectfully decline your request for _____.

Sincerely,

Your signature

Your full name
Home-Based Private
Educational Program Administrator

RESPONDING TO UNANNOUNCED CONTACT BY A SCHOOL OFFICIAL

If a school official contacts you unexpectedly:

--Do not panic. Given your careful preparatory work, you have every reason to feel confident. Stay calm. Take time to think. Remember, too, that the burden of proof is on the state to prove that you are not complying with the law and that the state needs to abide by rules of due process. (See pp. 222-224.)

--Be polite. On the phone or at the door (it may well be best not to invite the school official into your home, at least at first), explain that you are busy teaching your child, that you know the law and are in full compliance (again assuming of course that you are) and that you have discussed this, for example, with your local school superintendent and your legislators. If the official has further questions, ask her to submit them to you in writing or make an appointment to talk with you at a convenient time. Remember that you should read and interpret the laws yourself and you do not have to do more than the law requires.

If the official insists on talking with you right then, decide what seems best to do. Among the alternatives are the following:

--If you have done the preventive work outlined above and know you have at least some support (from your local school superintendent, for example) and perhaps even know the visiting official, it may be best in the long run to cooperate by inviting him in and showing him your daily attendance records (which will document your compliance with the compulsory school attendance law). Perhaps he is under pressure from other people and with this kind of cooperation from you, he will be able to satisfy their concerns. If he wants a copy of your attendance record and you are willing to cooperate, offer to make a copy yourself and send it to him; do not give him the original. Be aware, however, that many home schoolers have found that when they tried to cooperate with a school official by doing more than the law requires, the official then requested even more, criticized the home schooler, or used against the home schooler the information that she had volunteered. Therefore some home schoolers do not invite school officials into their homes.

--If the official is not satisfied with just seeing your attendance records, you may want to talk further with him about your program. (Before agreeing to this, remember that the experience of many home schoolers has been that officials are usually looking for problems rather than successes. They have been trained to behave in a bureaucratic and legalistic manner, and they often do not understand the law, parental rights in education, or the principles of due process.)

You may want to tape the conversation. Begin by having each person present identify himself or herself and acknowledge that a tape is being made. You may want to have a witness present--a neighbor, for example.

Think seriously before voluntarily showing the official anything that is not required by law, since this could set a precedent. Also, home school curriculums that differ from those used in public schools tend to raise more questions in an official's mind than they answer. Remember that you do not have to prove your compliance with the law. You are talking with him in the spirit of cooperation. It may be better not to discuss areas that are not mentioned in the law, which may include your educational background, income level, textbook selection, etc. Do not be intimidated; feel free to stick with an answer you want to give, no matter how many times you have to repeat it. Silence can also be effective if you do not want to discuss something. Remember that you can end the conversation if you want to.

--As another alternative, if the official seems somewhat less than friendly, you can refuse to talk and refuse to let her in.

If the official does leave and then sends you a letter, respond but remember you do not have to give more information than the law requires. If an interview is set up, some of the above suggestions may be helpful.

RESPONDING TO CONTACT BY A SOCIAL SERVICE WORKER

Home schoolers are seldom contacted by social service workers. However, because such contacts can have serious consequences, the following comments and suggestions are included.

256

In most states, a county or state social service worker has legal authority to intervene in the life of a family on the basis on a complaint. (The family will not necessarily know the source of the complaint.) Such a worker can question parents and children without needing to have formal evidence or an indictment. Results of such questioning can be serious, including removing a child from his home. Therefore contacts by social service workers need to be taken very seriously and handled carefully. For example, if a parent refuses to let a social service worker in, the worker can quickly (in a matter of minutes or a few hours) get a warrant which requires the parent to admit her. For this reason, some parents feel it is better to allow a social service worker who requests admission to come in, rather than complicate the situation by appearing to hide something and thereby raising the stakes of the visit.

Usually if a home schooler is suspected of failing to comply with the home schooling law, the case is handled by a truant officer. However, a social service worker who is investigating a family for other reasons may begin asking questions about their home school. It may be best for home schoolers to try to keep home schooling separate from whatever other investigations are being conducted. If this is impossible, parents may want to point out that home schooling is providing important benefits for their child.

If a home schooler is contacted by a social service worker, he may find it helpful to discuss this with other home schoolers in a support group and/or a state organization.

RECORDING CONTACTS WITH PUBLIC OFFICIALS

Whatever the outcome of your contact with a public official, record it. This documentation is important for several reasons. First, if the contact develops into an adversarial situation, documentation will be important. Second, documentation will help others who are assisting you. (These may include friends, other home schoolers, the media, your legislator, an attorney, etc.) Third, a home schooling organization may want to establish a record of case histories of home schoolers who are contacted by various people. Your documentation will help this organization be effective in dealing with the state department of education, the legislature, and the media. Fourth, documentation shows officials that they are dealing with a person who knows his rights under the law and who will be thorough in dealing with other people and agencies. This may deter officials who might otherwise try to take advantage of a situation without due cause, but it does not upset officials who are on solid, professional footing.

It is wise to document conversations with local school officials, state education officials, district attorneys' offices, the media, etc. In addition to the content of your conversation, include such information as its date, time, and location and whether it was in person or by telephone. If anyone else was present, give his name, title, employer, and position.

PRESCHOOL SCREENING

Preschool screening and placement are areas in which it is crucial for parents to assume responsibility. Most states do not require preschool screening by statute or regulation, but school districts' letters and literature on the subject may clearly give the impression that it is required. Actually, if a public or private school receives federal funding for special education, it must make its programs, including testing and screening, available to all children. However, participation is voluntary. It would be helpful to parents if screening announcements said something like, "We are required to inform you that free preschool screening is available for all children ages __ to __. Your child's participation in this screening is voluntary. If you are interested, please contact..." But this might jeopardize the jobs of testers and school personnel who often have a strong self-interest and financial interest in finding children with special needs.

Serious consideration should be given to the harm done by preschool testing. Inaccurate results can be generated when evaluators make errors during testing, invent problems where none exists, confuse children, deny the acceptability of developmental differences, use a stressful testing environment that interferes with a child's performance or ability to cooperate, etc. Such inaccurate results may damage a child's self-esteem. As self-fulfilling prophecies, they may also lead to long term problems.

What is really happening in a preschool screening? Educational bureaucracies and professional special interest groups are deciding what qualities, abilities, and skill levels are important and must be demonstrated by a preschooler in order for her to be labeled "normal." But what about families who value qualities different from those chosen by the government bureaucracy? What about a child who is developing well but on a schedule different from the one prescribed? A sensitive child who is too overwhelmed by strangers in new surroundings to demonstrate her real abilities? A "genius" who just does not fit the expected patterns?

Questions can also be raised about the wisdom of using "professional experts" to assess a child's strengths and limitations when parents have a wealth of information and are the real experts concerning their own child. Such assessments require careful observation, which concerned and loving parents do well. Although a big mystique has developed around the process of diagnosing and labeling all sorts of alleged disorders, most of it is based on either common sense or unsubstantiated theories. Serious problems are pretty obvious, and some less serious problems that are diagnosed turn out, on closer examination, to be ridiculous.

Numerous articles and books have been written on the problems with the diagnostic methods and techniques used to identify children with "exceptional educational needs" and "learning disabilities." Gerald S. Coles' *Learning Mystique* is a comprehensive study of the research and literature on "learning

259

disabilities." Coles concludes that there is no reliable method or technique for identifying "learning disabilities." Lori and Bill Granger's *Magic Feather* documents the damage labels do to children and the growth of programs for "learning disabled" students in response to federal and state funding. Thomas Armstrong's *In Their Own Way* and Frank Smith's *Insult to Intelligence* demonstrate the severe limitations of the learning theory that supports most "special education." Holt Associates' *Everyone Is Able* provides valuable perspective on how children get labeled and what parents can do about it.

The criticism is not limited to theorists, writers, and psychiatrists. LaVaun Dennett, Principal at Montlake Elementary School in Seattle's inner city, has removed learning disabled labels, mainstreamed special education teachers and students, and given up federal funds. The experiment has been a great success. Children have made remarkable achievement gains. Teachers have gained greater autonomy. Parents want their children placed in this inner city school. Businesses are very supportive. The "no labels" experiment has been expanded to 21 other schools. The Washington state legislature is working to support this approach.

But some parents wonder, "Why not have my child tested just to be sure he is all right? I can do whatever I want with the results of the tests." There are several problems with this approach:

--Regardless of what one knows about the inaccuracy and unreliability of test results, it is extremely difficult not to be influenced by them, especially since they are presented in such "scientific" terms by "professional experts."

--Preschool testing begins or extends a record on your child that could end up following her for a long time. Should the state have questionable information and test results from the preschool years, especially from ages to which the compulsory school attendance law does not apply? It does seem reasonable for federal and state aid to be available for children who have obvious and serious problems and whose parents request such aid. But this is an example of taking an idea that may have some merit for a few children and applying it to all children.

--The more people who participate in such screenings, the more power and credibility are given to the "experts." This can also contribute to an attempt to make screening mandatory rather than voluntary.

--Relying on preschool screening robs parents of the confidence-building experience of making their own assessments and judgments based on their own observations and decisions about what is important.

If you receive a letter from your school district announcing preschool screening or telling you to report for it, you can respond in one of several ways.

--You can assume responsibility for deciding for yourself whether your preschooler's development is within acceptable limits. To do this, you need to observe your child, which you are no doubt already doing. Serious problems are generally obvious. If you feel you need more background information, try a book like Frank Smith's *Reading Without Nonsense*. He points out that:

Children who have learned to comprehend spoken language (not necessarily the language of school, but some language that makes sense in the world they live in) and who can see sufficiently well to distinguish a pin from a paper clip on the table in front of them have already demonstrated sufficient language, visual acuity, and learning ability to learn how to read. (p. 9)

Many parents find it helpful to keep records of their child's learning and activities so they can see progress more clearly. A discussion with someone who knows your child and shares your values, perspectives, and approach to education can also be helpful.

--You can then ignore a letter like the one above, since you know the law, your rights under it, and your child's abilities.

261

--You can let others in your community know the facts in this matter.

--You can also ask the author of such a letter to document his statements with legal references or issue a retraction or clarification.

FORMS NOT REQUIRED BY LAW

Occasionally school districts send forms to home schoolers requesting information not required by law. Home schoolers should think seriously before filling out such forms or supplying similar information to local school officials or other public officials. This is important because:

--Your providing information sets a precedent. Any time a citizen gives a bureaucracy more information than is required by law, the bureaucracy's power and control are increased. By their nature, bureaucracies grow and spread. One of the most effective ways they do this is by repeatedly asking for small, seemingly harmless pieces of information. If citizens comply without giving the matter much thought, before long the bureaucracy may have gathered an impressive amount of information. More importantly, the practice can turn into a legal claim over you that will be extremely difficult to change. It is important for citizens to resist this encroachment on their rights and liberties.

--Although the information you provide may seem innocent and insignificant, it may be used to support a claim by local public school officials that they should have (or actually do have) more authority over home schoolers. Sometimes supplying a piece of information can legally be construed as an indication that a bureaucracy has authority over the individual supplying the information. Or it can be used as a justification for the bureaucracy's demanding such authority.

Home schoolers should also exercise caution in responding to requests for information about their home school from researchers working for the state department of education, a university, or any other organization. Such information can end up being distorted, misinterpreted, quoted out of context, and misused. For more information on the problems of research, see Chapter 18.

If you have any questions about a form or other request for information that you have received from a public official, or if you need help dealing with such a request, discuss this with other home schoolers in your support group or state home schooling organization.

CHAPTER 26

WORKING WITH PUBLIC SCHOOLS

PROBLEM SOLVING THROUGH EFFECTIVE COMMUNICATION WITH PUBLIC SCHOOL OFFICIALS

Sometimes it benefits both home schoolers and public schools to work together, as in the case of "shared services". (The term "shared services" refers to participation in public school classes and other activities by students not enrolled full time in that particular school.) Other times, as in the case of entry/re-entry, home schoolers enrolling their children in a public school have to work with school officials. In such cases, the following steps may help. Once this approach has been used for one issue, it is easier to use it in succeeding cases.

(1)--Do background research. Find out what current policy is. Be prepared to talk with several different people before you find someone who can answer your questions fully. If possible, track the policy to its source. If it is a written policy, get an exact copy. If it is not written, find out as much as you can about the policy from the people responsible for enforcing it. If you are told that something is "required by law," get the number of the statute and then get a copy of the statute itself, either from the person with whom you are speaking, your local library, or your legislator.

(2)--Network with other home schoolers to answer the following questions:

--What is your goal? What policy or outcome do you want?

--What factual evidence and supporting arguments can you use to convince people to accept your approach?

--How would your proposal benefit the other party (such as the public school)? It is very important to view the situation from the perspective of the other side. The more you can convince them of ways in which your proposal will benefit them, or solve problems for them, the better chance you have that it will be adopted.

--If you are working to change existing policy or if the problem you are working on is covered by statute, be sure to read and interpret these policies or statutes yourself. Often, people with the most at stake have the clearest, most reasonable perspective, despite the commonly held notion that they are not "objective" enough. Do not accept anyone else's interpretations, even if they are the basis of years of practice. Just because a person is getting paid to interpret or enforce a policy does not mean he is right. One of our greatest strengths as home schoolers is our experience with alternative perspectives and practices. Use your expertise in this area. For more information on reading and interpreting laws, see pp. 197-201.

(3)--Have your policy or approach accepted.

--Present your proposal and supporting arguments reasonably and politely to the appropriate person. If you need the approval of a group, such as your school board, meet with individual members first, beginning with the one you expect to be most supportive of your ideas. Contact each of them individually before asking to make a presentation before the group.

--Include in your presentation factual information that will help other people feel comfortable about home schooling in general. Be polite, reasonable, and as conventional as possible. Stick to the issue under discussion.

--If you reach an impasse before you reach agreement, ask yourself and your adversary what other alternatives exist that might be acceptable. (Remember that you are good at dealing with alternatives.) Do not be afraid to suggest new ideas that may at first seem impossible.

--Once a positive policy is in place, do all you can to see that you and other home schoolers act responsibly in accord with it.

Developing a good working relationship with your local school board can pay big dividends. Consider, for example, what happened when one school board acted in support of home schoolers, as described in Mary Penn's article "Board nixes home school monitoring," which appeared in the *Sauk Prairie Star*, Sauk Prairie, WI, on October 26, 1989. Ms. Penn reported on the discussion that followed the introduction of a resolution "which would have enabled school district personnel to visit and evaluate local home schooling situations."

Board member Tony DeGiovanni said, "Personally I do not think we need to take on that responsibility. I don't know how a person would evaluate a home school. If the state wants them to follow guidelines, I think that is their problem. I think we are ill prepared to measure what is going on in a home school."

Board member Walter Dickey said the philosophy of home schooling is not to educate so students can pass certain tests, so standardized testing could prove meaningless in a home schooling situation. "If the state feels it is a problem they should legislate it," Dickey said.

"If it is not a big problem, say four to five students go to the high school and are not at grade level, I think they should leave it alone," DeGiovanni said.

Val McAuliffe objected to what she sees as the "inflammatory" wording of the resolution. McAuliffe said any movement to home schooling means the district has its own education problems to deal with.

266

The resolution died for lack of a motion. (Reprinted with permission.)

ENTRY/RE-ENTRY

The question of the entry or re-entry of a former home schooler into a conventional school may cause concern among a variety of people for different reasons.

--Many home schoolers eventually enter or re-enter a conventional school. Their parents, of course, want to be sure that they are as well prepared as possible and that the transition goes smoothly.

--School officials who are critical or skeptical of home schooling sometimes allude to problems home schoolers may cause if they enter conventional schools. These concerns are vague and are not documented, simply because there have been no significant problems although thousands of children enter or re-enter public schools from home schools each year.

--School districts sometimes pass entry policies that discriminate against home schoolers.

HELPING YOUR CHILD ENTER/RE-ENTER A CONVENTIONAL SCHOOL

Many parents whose children have entered school have found the following suggestions helpful:

--At least several months before your child will enter school, begin establishing a good working relationship with school personnel. Visit the school, sit in on classes, and talk with teachers and the principal. Being familiar with the facilities is often reassuring to a child; and you can ask about policies concerning records, credits, tests, and psychological counseling and screening.

267

You can also request further information from the district superintendent and the school board. It is particularly important to find out how your child's grade placement will be determined. Among the questions to ask: What criteria will be used? (Among the possibilities are age, test results, curriculum, review of the child's record and credits, interview of the child and parent, determination of social maturity.) Which of these is most important and/or mandatory? Which could be waived or de-emphasized? Who makes the final decision? Decide if the criteria are reasonable, non-discriminatory, and acceptable to you.

--Try to change discriminatory or questionable policies and procedures or have them waived. For suggestions, see below.

--Some schools require that entering students take standardized tests. This is a discriminatory policy if it is not applied to all students; see below for more details. Some parents object to standardized tests for entering students and work hard to prevent their child's having to take them. If tests are unavoidable, some parents arrange to have them administered in a setting in which the child is comfortable and to stay with younger children. Sometimes the tests can be postponed until the child has been in school for several months. Many parents also find it beneficial to have their child practice taking sample tests of the same type from the same company as those she will take at school.

--Be careful about signing any authorizations or waivers, especially concerning psychological testing and screening procedures. Some controversial tests cannot be administered without parental permission, and it is important to find out exactly what test will be administered, why, and what will be done with the results before signing away rights that are yours and your child's.

--Many parents work hard to give their child extra support as he is adjusting to school. They communicate frequently with his teacher(s), offer to help with homework, and act as their child's advocate whenever necessary. Extra time and effort often pay big dividends in a smooth transition and good adjustment for their child.

DEALING WITH ENTRY/RE-ENTRY POLICIES OF LOCAL SCHOOL BOARDS

(1) Are formal entry/re-entry policies a good idea or necessary?

No. Schools are able to place home schooled children easily, usually on the basis of age. Obviously, everyone involved (child, parents, administrator, teachers, and school) will be best served if the child is appropriately placed, and a flexible, case-by-case approach seems most likely to produce this result. Detailed entry policies are not needed and in some cases cause problems. (Many schools do not use test results to determine placement.)

(2) Why do some school districts have formal entry policies?

The state department of education (possibly in response to demands from teachers unions) sometimes encourages districts to adopt such policies, allegedly to ensure uniformity throughout the state and provide an indirect means of controlling and regulating home schooling.

Some districts adopt such policies because they think they might need them sometime, because they have been told other districts have them, and/or because these policies supposedly deter home schooling. If no one challenges such policies when they are proposed, they are often passed for lack of opposition.

Basically these policies exist because school personnel and school boards do not understand home schooling. It does not seem possible to them that parents could teach their own children, or if it is possible, it is an alternative they find unsettling.

(3) On what basis should home schoolers evaluate proposed entry policies?

If home schoolers cannot convince their local school board that a formal entry policy is unnecessary, they need to be sure that any policy which is adopted does not discriminate against home schoolers. This means that the only valid requirements for entry of home schoolers are those which are also required for entry of other transfer students (whether from public or other private schools) and for promotion of students from one grade to the next within the school. Examples of specific requirements which are sometimes placed exclusively on home schoolers are:

--Achievement of a certain score or percentile on a standardized test in order to be placed in a given grade.

--Completion of a probationary period during which a former home schooler must prove herself.

--Demonstration of social maturity, including a certain degree of socialization or appropriate interaction with peers.

--Enrollment by a certain chronological age, after which entry is denied.

--Completion of a certain number of semesters at the school to be eligible for a diploma.

(4) What arguments can be used against discriminatory policies?

--There is no concrete evidence that such discrimination against home schoolers is necessary. Thousands of former home schoolers have entered or re-entered conventional schools without significant problems, and the need for such strict and unreasonable policies has not been demonstrated.

--State constitutions require that public schools provide services for all children and not deny them on the basis of discriminatory practices.

--The fourteenth amendment of the U.S. Constitution guarantees equal treatment under the law and protects citizens against discrimination. (For more details, see pp. 223.)

--Such policies violate the principle of "innocent until proven guilty" by assuming there is something wrong with home schoolers until they have proven otherwise. Some policies also disregard due process.

(5) How can home schoolers work to prevent or correct discriminatory and unfavorable entry policies?

--Be informed about the activities of you local school board so that whenever possible you can work to prevent the passage of these policies. Prevention is usually easier than changing an existing policy.

--Follow the steps outlined in "Problem Solving Through Effective Communication with Public School Officials" above. Throughout, stick to the topic of entry policy; do not get drawn into general discussions about the validity of home schooling or reports on the activities of individual families. Be positive about home schooling; do not criticize or attack the public schools. Specific actions which may be helpful include: writing to school officials and school board members; meeting with individual members of the board and with the school superintendent before meeting with the board as a whole; building a documented record to demonstrate discriminatory practices; and using the media by writing letters to the local paper and requesting that it cover the formation of entry policy as a news story.

--Be positive and optimistic. Home schoolers in a number of school districts have been able to stop the passage of proposed entry policies that were discriminatory and unfavorable.

SHARED SERVICES: PARTICIPATION OF HOME SCHOOLERS IN PUBLIC SCHOOLS

The term "shared services" refers to participation in public school classes and other activities by students not enrolled full time in that particular school. This includes home schoolers, other private school students, and students from other public schools. Some home schoolers may be interested in shared services so they

271

can take a course of special interest, such as advanced math, or one requiring specialized equipment, such as a science lab; participate in a group activity such as chorus, band, or a team sport; enroll in a summer school program; gain personal experience in a public school setting; or take driver education.

If you are interested in shared services, these suggestions may be of help.

(1) Following the general steps in "Problem Solving Through Effective Communication With Public School Officials" on pp. 264-266, find out the policy of your local school. Some schools already have shared services available, so you only have to ask. Sometimes you can convince a school administrator to let your child take one course without needing to wait for the school or district to establish a formal policy. (Some of the points in (2) below may help.) If you do this, realize that you have a responsibility; the way you and your child act will have a strong impact on the response given to the next home schooler with a similar request. After one or more positive experiences, you may be in a good position to ask the school and/or district to institute a formal policy of shared services for home schoolers. (If common practice were not so far removed from constitutional and statutory provisions, you would not need to go through these steps to reclaim parental and children's rights in education. See below for more on this.)

(2) However, many school administrators react negatively to the idea of shared services for home schoolers. Do not take an initial refusal personally and do not give up (unless you decide shared services are not that important after all). Administrators may be suspicious of home schoolers in general, too busy to tackle one more program, concerned about the number of people who will come flocking to their doors, uninterested in trying a new idea, or simply tired and overworked. School personnel may say something like:

--The incorrect statement, "It is all or nothing," meaning that only full-time students may participate in school activities. In fact, part-time participation is legal and has many precedents in most states, including three, four, and five year olds, summer school students, home-bound students, and students enrolled in private schools who participate in special education courses funded by the government in either public or private schools. Also, some states count students on a "full-time equivalent" basis which means prorating part-time students based on the number of courses or hours they attend.

--The incorrect statement, "It would cost too much money." See below for ideas about how school districts can get money for part-time students. In addition, public schools are required by law to serve everyone, an obligation they cannot avoid because of cost.

--The unfriendly charge, "You are the competition." In fact, a public school official is a public servant obligated by law to serve parents and children. He is not supposed to be a monopolistic businessperson competing with home schooling parents for students.

Following step 2 in "Problem Solving Through Effective Communication With Public School Officials" above, network with other home schoolers in your district. If your local school resists your participation in shared services, the best strategy may be to try to convince the school board to adopt a policy that encourages shared services. Be sure to consider the position of the school and the school board (as well as your own) in making your case--you will have a better chance of convincing them if you can show that such a policy will benefit them as well as you. Among the arguments you can use are:

--Economic: Administrators often argue that shared services are too expensive, especially if they can claim that the school does not receive state aid for such students. We are not arguing that a school should receive full-time state aid for a student who is attending only part-time. But public schools sometimes receive state aid for part-time students, such as summer school students. You may be able to help your school or district negotiate with the state so they can get proportional funding for home schoolers. Ideally, you should not have to help find the means by which funding is forthcoming. Yet, your participating in this way may help schools move to serving parents and children again, rather than serving bureaucracies.

However, even if your district cannot get state aids for your child's participation, do not accept the argument that there is not enough money in the local school district budget for your child to take a course. Most districts deal with much larger unexpected demands for courses and money than home schoolers ever make.

--Community relations: The more people the schools can involve in their programs, the more support from the community they will have.

--Legal: State constitutions and/or statutes require that public schools make educational programs available to all children.

--Improved communication and cooperation among those working with children: The more communication and cooperation there is among adults who are involved in educating children, the better will be the educational opportunities available to all children.

In planning your strategy, remember that the school administrator or school board will be more likely to be receptive to your request if you are as cooperative as possible. Acknowledge that the request you are making may require extra planning and work for the school. Offer to help minimize this work or get it done. Also indicate your support for the public schools, or at least for the programs in which your child wants to participate. Some school officials assume all home schoolers are against public schools.

USING YOUR STATE'S OPEN RECORDS LAW

When dealing with state and local school officials and other public officials, you may sometimes find it helpful to use the federal freedom of information act and your state's equivalent to this act, sometimes referred to as open records laws, which guarantee public access to public documents.

This might be important if public officials are doing research or surveys that impact on home schoolers or collecting stories or anecdotal evidence about home schoolers, especially if there is reason to think that these stories may be one-sided and present only negative evidence. You can use the open records law to gain access to files, documents produced by public officials (including reports they have written), and letters sent to them (such as reports from neighbors). Then you can work to correct inaccurate or misleading information, to provide balance or clarification, or to plan other strategies for dealing with the situation.

However, even though you have a legal right to these public documents, you should realize that a public official may react negatively or resist providing the information. She may not be accustomed to being subject to these statutes and may not even be aware of the openness they require. Therefore, in requesting public documents, it may help if you are polite but firm and cite or quote the statutes on which your request is based. Certain drafts of documents are not subject to this law. To protect the privacy of individuals and to comply with federal privacy laws, names and addresses may need to be removed from some documents before they are released.

CONCLUSION

WAYS YOU CAN ENSURE PERSONAL AND POLITICAL EMPOWERMENT

To help ensure personal and political empowerment and foster a positive climate for home schooling, you can:

--Make sure your own house is in order. Act in ways that will reflect positively on home schooling.

--Know your rights and responsibilities under the law. Understand the legal, moral, practical, and historical arguments that support home schooling.

--Communicate with other home schoolers. Become involved in a local support group and a state-wide grassroots organization. If necessary, organize them yourself.

--Remain united with other home schoolers. We need to work together to protect our rights and freedom to home school. We can learn from each other as we accept individual differences in areas such as choice of curriculum, approaches to learning, and beliefs and principles.

--Become acquainted with educational issues in your community. Attend one or two local school board meetings, not necessarily to discuss home schooling but to learn how the board operates and what its concerns are.

--Learn about problems public schools are facing and how they are being handled. Our society has asked and is continuing to ask a lot of our public schools. We may not agree with everything they do, but we need to understand them as best we can. Do not attack the public schools.

--Set the right kind of precedents. Acting to prevent or correct seemingly small infringements on our rights may prevent larger problems. Resist the temptation to use personal credentials ("I am a certified teacher") or status ("I am recognized as an exemplary home schooler"), even to get out of a difficult situation with a school official, reporter, etc. Using credentials or status may make it difficult for other home schoolers who do not have the same credentials or status (which are not necessary for home schooling anyway).

--Get to know your legislators. Legislators need to view home schoolers as individuals and families, not just names and numbers. The able work we do in educating our children and our commitment to this effort can best be communicated through personal contact. A legislator is less likely to view home schoolers merely as a political faction if he knows us as individuals.

--Do not assume someone else is going to identify and solve a problem. Each of us needs to be alert to what is happening that affects or could affect home schooling at the community and state level. State grassroots organizations learn of important events from individual home schoolers, not through some top-down chain of command. Establish and use communication channels to help us all be informed.

--But do not act hastily on your own. Before making a move, particularly on an important issue, discuss your concerns and proposed strategy with other home schoolers. Without this kind of communication, we could easily make serious mistakes or work at cross-purposes, threatening each other's effectiveness.

--Promote a positive image of home schooling through newspaper articles, letters to the editor, comments on radio talk shows, etc.

--Accentuate the positive. Celebrate and give thanks for your family, for what you are able to do. Take time to let your children's presence invigorate you and show you why the work is worthwhile.

APPENDIX A

RESOURCES FOR HOME SCHOOLERS

NATIONAL PUBLICATIONS AND ORGANIZATIONS

Home schoolers come from all walks of life and choose to home school for a variety of reasons. Home schooling publishers, newsletters, book stores, and curriculum vendors reflect different approaches to home schooling. We offer a description of each of the following publications and/or organizations in an effort to give you some general idea how each may relate to your main interests and approach to education. The descriptions are generalizations which do not do justice to the complexity of each organization. Undoubtedly they have each served a wide variety of home schoolers. Information from these sources will give you many ideas for additional reading and other resources.

--*Growing Without Schooling*--Founded in 1977 by the late John Holt, this bimonthly magazine is now published by Holt Associates, Inc. It features ideas and experiences of home schoolers, interviews, book reviews, resources, and a national directory of home schoolers and their supporters. Holt Associates also operate a mail order book and music store. This organization addresses alternative approaches to learning and educational issues. (2269 Massachusetts Avenue, Cambridge, MA 02140)

--*Home Education Magazine*--Founded in 1983 by the current publishers, Mark and Helen Hegener, this bimonthly publication includes regular columnists and feature articles. The Hegeners also operate Home Education Press and a mail order book store. The organization provides a forum for a variety of approaches to home schooling rather than a decided educational or ideological point of view. It sees itself as a bridge or unifying agent within the home schooling movement. (Post Office Box 1083, Tonasket, WA 98855)

--*The Moore Report*--Founded in 1989 by Raymond and Dorothy Moore as a continuation of their many years of work in home schooling, this newsletter reports on research, offers support for home schooling, and provides a forum for exchanging ideas. The Moores strongly support delayed formal instruction and have a non-exclusionary Christian perspective. (Post Office Box 1, Camas, WA 98607)

--*The National Homeschool Association*--Founded in 1989, this organization's purpose is "to advocate individual choice and freedom in education, to serve those families who choose to homeschool, and to inform the general public about home education." The NHA is inclusive and grassroots in character, operates through an elected council, and emphasizes consensus in decision making. It provides a national information network, a quarterly "Circle of Correspondence" publication, and an annual conference as well as giving general home schooling information to interested parties. (Post Office Box 58746, Seattle, WA 98138-1746)

BOOKS

Here are a few suggestions, not an exhaustive list. Some of these books have recommendations for further reading and information about curriculums and learning materials. Also see the resource list covering high school and after on pp. 80-83.

(1) IDEAS ABOUT LEARNING. Although these books do not deal directly with home schooling as such, many home schoolers find their ideas very helpful.

--Armstrong, Thomas. *In Their Own Way: Discovering and Encouraging Your Child's Personal Learning Style*. Los Angeles: Jeremy P. Tarcher, 1987.

--Holt, John. *How Children Learn*, Revised Edition. NY: Delacourte, 1967, 1983.

_____. *Learning All the Time*. Reading, MA: Addison-Wesley, 1989.

--Moore, Raymond and Dorothy Moore. *Better Late Than Early*. NY: Reader's Digest, 1975.

--Smith, Frank. *Joining the Literacy Club: Further Essays into Education*. Portsmouth, NH: Heinemann, 1988.

_____. *Reading Without Nonsense*. Second Edition. NY: Teachers College Press, 1985.

(2) GENERAL BOOKS ABOUT HOME SCHOOLING.

--Arons, Stephen. *Compelling Belief: The Culture of American Schooling*. NY: McGraw-Hill, 1983.

--Hegener, Mark and Helen, Eds. *The Home School Reader*. Tonasket, WA: Home Education Press, 1988.

--Holt, John. *Teach Your Own: A Hopeful Path for Education*. NY: Delacorte, 1981.

--Moore, Raymond. *Home Grown Kids*. Albuquerque, NM: World Books, 1981.

--Petersen, Anne, and Peggy O'Mara, Eds. *Schooling at Home: Parents, Kids, and Learning.* Santa Fe: John Muir, 1990.

--Pride, Mary. *The New Big Book of Home Learning.* Westchester, IL: Crossway Books, 1988.

_____. *The Next Big Book of Home Learning.* Westchester, IL: Crossway Books, 1987.
(Note: Mary Pride's books are being revised into a four volume set.)

--Reed, Donn. *The First Home-School Catalog.* Second Edition, Revised. Lyndon, VT: Brook Farm Books.

(3) BOOKS BASED ON THE PERSONAL HOME SCHOOLING EXPERIENCES OF THE AUTHOR. Some include general suggestions and resources.

--Colfax, David and Micki. *Homeschooling for Excellence.* Philo, CA: Mountain House Press, 1987.

--Joudry, Patricia. *...and the children played.* Montreal: Tundra Books, 1975.

--Richman, Howard and Susan. *The Three R's at Home.* Kittanning, PA: Pennsylvania Homeschoolers, 1988.

--Wallace, Nancy. *Better than School.* Burdett, NY: Larson, 1983.

BIBLIOGRAPHY of publications cited in this book.

Armstrong, Thomas. *In Their Own Way: Discovering and Encouraging Your Child's Personal Learning Style.* Los Angeles: Jeremy P. Tarcher, 1987.

Brooks, Mona. *Drawing With Children*. Los Angeles: Jeremy P. Tarcher, Inc., 1986.

Carnegie Forum on Education and the Economy. *A Nation Prepared: Teachers for the 21st Century*. 1986.

Coles, Gerald S. *The Learning Mystique: A Critical Look at "Learning Disabilities."* NY: Pantheon Books, 1987.

Diehl, Kathryn and G. K. Hodenfield. *Johnny STILL Can't Read-- But You Can Teach Him at Home*. Scottsdale, AZ: Reading Reform Foundation.

Elias. Stephen. *Legal Research: How to Find and Understand the Law*. Berkeley, CA: Nolo Press, 1982.
Granger, Lori and Bill. *The Magic Feather: The Truth about "Special Education."* NY: Dutton, 1986.

Hanushek, Eric A. "The Economics of Schooling: Production and Efficiency in Public Schools." *Journal of Economic Literature*, Vol. 24 (Sept., 1986), pp. 1141-1177.

Henderson, Anne T., Ed. *The Evidence Continues to Grow: Parent Involvement Improves Student Achievement*. Columbia, MD: National Committee for Citizens in Education, 1987.

Holt, John. *How Children Learn*, Revised Edition. NY: Delacourte, 1967, 1983.

_____. *Learning All the Time*. Reading, MA: Addison-Wesley, 1989.

_____. *Teach Your Own: A Hopeful Path for Education*. NY: Delacorte, 1981.

Holt Associates, Inc. *Everyone Is Able: Exploding The Myth of Learning Disabilities*. Cambridge, MA: Holt Associates, 1987.

Kobrin, Beverly. *Eyeopeners! How to Choose and Use Children's Books About Real People, Places and Things*. NY: Penguin Books, 1988.

Smith, Frank. *Insult to Intelligence: The Bureaucratic Invasion of Our Classrooms*. NY: Arbor House, 1986.

_____. *Joining the Literacy Club: Further Essays into Education*. Portsmouth, NH: Heinemann, 1988.

_____. *Reading Without Nonsense*. Second Edition. NY: Teachers College Press, 1985.

Trelease, Jim. *The Read-Aloud Handbook*. NY: Penguin, 1982.

Using a Law Library. Published by HALT, Inc., An Organization of Americans for Legal Reform, 1319 F Street NW, Washington, DC 20004, 1983.

Whitehead, John W. and Wendell R. Bird. *Home Education and Constitutional Liberties: The Historical and Constitutional Arguments in Support of Home Instruction*. Westchester, IL: Crossway Books, 1984.

INDEX

INDEX

LARRY and SUSAN KASEMAN have been working together since they met under an umbrella in 1966. Among the results are a marriage, a family that includes four remarkable children with whom they have been home schooling since the oldest finished first grade in 1979, a commitment to alternatives and to simple living, and this book. Both are actively involved in Wisconsin Parents Association, a grassroots home schooling organization. As individuals, Larry has also been a bureaucrat and a small businessman while Susan has focused on mothering, nurturing, cooking whole foods, and knitting. They now live in an old farm house near Stoughton, Wisconsin.

For additional copies of this book,
please send $12.95 for each book to
Koshkonong Press
2545 Koshkonong Road
Stoughton, WI 53589

Add $2.00 for shipping
and handling.